Trout
maverick

Books by Leonard M. Wright, Jr.

Fishing the Dry Fly as a Living Insect (1972)

Fly Fishing Heresies (1975)

Where the Fish Are (1978)

The Masters on the Nymph (ed., with J. M. Migel, 1979)

The Ways of Trout (1985)

The Field & Stream Treasury of Trout Fishing (ed., 1986)

First Cast (1987)

Superior Flies (1989)

The Fly Fisher's Reader (ed., 1990)

Stonefly and Caddis Fly-Fishing (1991)

Neversink (1991)

Trout Maverick (1996)

Trout
maverick

Fly-Fishing
Heresies
and Tactics

Leonard M. Wright, Jr.

LYONS & BURFORD, PUBLISHERS

Printed in the United States of America

10 9 8 7 6 5 4 3 2 1

Design by LaBreacht Design

Library of Congress Cataloging-in-Publication Data

Wright, Leonard M.

    Trout maverick : fly-fishing heresies and tactics / Leonard M. Wright, Jr.

      p.   cm.

    ISBN 1-55821-476-3

    1. Trout fishing. 2. Fly fishing I. Title

    SH687.W745   1996

    799.1'755—dc20   96-12461

                                      CIP

Some of this material has appeared previously in *American Sportsman, The Anglers' Club Bulletin, Field & Stream, Fishing World, Fly Fisherman, Gray's Sporting Journal, Outdoor Life,* and *Sports Afield.*

contents

preface

A few of the chapters in this book were written at least twenty-five years ago and I have included them without rewriting them, but only adding a brief introduction to each. That's because I find the information and theories they contain are just as accurate, helpful, or innovative as they were when I first wrote them down.

Note carefully, I don't use either the word "discover" or "invent" although I did get many of these ideas from independent observation and did, at the time, feel they were original. With my current 20/20 hindsight I now realize that this can't possibly be the case. Some other fly fishermen surely must have experimented and adopted similar tactics and techniques. But, as far as I know, they simply never bothered to write them up.

Fishing a dry fly with a slight, upstream twitch . . . tying floating caddis imitations with hackle-fiber wings . . . dancing a dropper down-current . . . using extra-long fly rods . . . and the conviction that wet flies are superior to nymphs—all are "heresies" I still firmly embrace.

The main reason why I seldom fish by the book (except, perhaps when spent mayflies are on the water) is that I've found that my unconventional tactics usually work better. I try to adapt my flies and presentations to what I actually see insects and trout do—or not do—rather than what the books say.

I started down this track when I tried to figure out how to catch trout when they were feeding on hatching or egg-laying adult caddisflies. I was forced into intense observation and brute logic—not because of any gift of genius or character—but because thirty years ago, there was virtually nothing in the fishing library on the subject.

Another influence on my off-beat techniques has been the rich history of fly fishing. After all, for hundreds of years, anglers in

Europe caught sophisticated brown trout with tackle and flies we now consider from the Stone Age. Were they doing things we have since thrown out or forgotten?

Dapping, dancing the dropper, and the use of far longer fly rods all fall into this category. All are, at best, borrowings (at worst, thefts) from the past and yet they are deadly on today's streams. Although I have written about them extensively, I have yet to encounter another angler astream who dapped, danced a dropper, or used a fly rod over nine feet long.

If my tactics and techniques are so oddball that I've earned the titles of "heretic" or "maverick," so be it. After all, I'm in pretty distinguished company. Martin Luther was branded a heretic. And Samuel Augustus Maverick (1813–1870) was not the rough, renegade cattleman of popular belief, but was (and you can look it up) a Yale-educated gentleman whose principal occupation was the practice of law.

—Leonard M. Wright, Jr.
1996

PART 1
the fish

1

The Perfect Fish

We call a flounder flat or a pickerel skinny
—but compared to what?
Compared to a trout, of course.

Although I had been a compulsive fisherman ever since I could walk, I never saw a specimen of "the perfect fish" until I had reached the advanced age of five and a half, going on six. I can still remember that moment. I was standing on a dusty dirt road, peering into a trickle—certainly not a brook—that dribbled out of a culvert, when I noticed a slight movement in the pan-sized pool below.

There couldn't be a fish in *there*, I thought. Fish, in those days were sudden shadows that disappeared in front of me as I waded through the shallows of seashores and lakes. Then a creature slowly assembled itself in front of my eyes. First, white-tipped pink fins fanning the yellow sand—probably the motion that had caught my eye in the first place. Then, below, a cigar-shaped shadow and above this a dark green body laced with paler markings. If I close my eyes today I can still see it in glorious full color, hovering there under the midday sun.

This was a fish I had never seen before—neither in the water, in picture books, nor in fish markets—yet I knew with utter certainly what it was. I had heard my father's friends talk in respectful tones about catching them on trips to Maine and Canada. This was a trout!

Admittedly, that six-incher was a Lilliputian sample, but it did qualify as "perfect." It was a member in good standing of a small, select group of closely related fish that offer the angler everything he could wish for. This elite list is limited to the flowing-water, insect-eating trouts and, as we shall see, only a few species carry all the necessary credentials.

The Atlantic salmon (*Salmo salar*) and its landlocked form, which is no longer considered a subspecies, deserve the place at the very top of this honor roll. Both spend major parts of their lives in running water and are really just large trout, as their first name, *Salmo*, indicates. They are mainly insectivorous during their lives in rivers and, even though the sea-run form does not feed at all during its return to fresh water, its insect-eating reflexes are reactivated at this time and it is usually caught on artificial flies.

The major species of what are usually called the trouts qualify, too, even though they may chase a lot of minnows and crayfish during the gluttony of old age. The brown trout (*Salmo trutta*) is an excellent example, feeding mostly on insects during its first five or six years of life and often after that when the supply is abundant. So does the rainbow (*Salmo gairdneri*) and the cutthroat (*Salmo clarki*). Taxonomists keep declaring (and undeclaring) new species and subspecies from time to time, but there's not much point in making finer distinctions as a fisherman.

Of the trout-cousins called chars, perhaps only the speckled (brook) trout (*Salvelinus fontinalis*) of the East qualifies. The Dolly Varden (*Salvelinus malma*) of the West Coast is not principally an insect feeder, nor is the arctic char (*Salvelinus alpinus*) of the North. The lake trout (*Salvelinus namaycush*) is unfortunately fond of deep water, and so are the several lesser-known chars of Europe.

Grayling, though they are even more distant relations of the true trouts, still deserve some consideration because they, too, sport the distinctive adipose fin of the tribe. They certainly prefer running water and they feed mainly on insects till they fall dead of old age. But, as we shall see, they fall short in other qualities and probably should be excluded. The Pacific salmons, six *Oncorhynchus* species, should be disqualified, too, since most are caught on heavy tackle in salt water and only a few are taken on insect imitations in fresh water.

From a scientific point of view, this grouping of fish by habits makes sense only to the angler. Scientists might further point out that the selected fish are not particularly smart, but merely shy, and that their place on the evolutionary ladder of fish is down near the bottom rung, far below the relatively advanced catfish. While I hold in great respect and awe any mental discipline that can put a man on the moon, I have to subtract a few points when it raises the catfish above the trout.

I am also aware that this selection may not exactly endear me to the army of trollers, surfers, bait-casters, or spin-fishers, either. In fact, I expect to hear accusations like "effete feather-fisherman," "trout chauvinist pig," or worse. And at this point, my chances of winning my case may seem as hopeless as Perry Mason's in the opening chapters. But stick around, there may be a surprise ending. I have a few expert witnesses and some devastating evidence.

First is the appraisal of history itself. Angling literature—which can boast of far more volumes than any other sport—has devoted more than half the pages in its library to this small group of fish. For every book that has been written about bass, pike, stripers, or sailfish, there are two, three, or more on salmon and trout, and most of the famous books—and the famous authors—throughout history have concentrated on these latter species.

Artists and illustrators seem to share this preoccupation with these same fish. Trout and salmon are drawn and painted more often than any other species. They are, that is, if you can disregard the stylized carp that appears on so many oriental plates and vases (and

I, for one, am perfectly willing to disqualify all crockery from the category of art).

A third field has also focused on this group of fish. Fish culturists have devoted, by far, the greater part of their efforts, both in research and in actual propagation, to trout and salmon. Habitat-improvement attempts have also dealt almost exclusively with bettering their streams and rivers. Today probably 80 percent of all hatcheries—I mean true hatcheries, not commercial fish farms—raise these fish exclusively.

How has this select group of fish managed to capture the imagination and inspire the efforts of the world of letters, art, and science for several centuries? And why have the trouts always been most prized by fishermen—at least in the countries where they occur in reasonable numbers? Simply because the list of virtues these fish possess is longer and more illustrious than the Boy Scout Oath.

The first quality that sets these fish apart is the manner in which they feed. To a very large extent, they subsist on insects and are readily caught on artificial imitations of these small, nutritious animals. Forgetting, for the moment, the joys and skills of fly tying, this preference in food makes delicate, sporting tackle not only possible but nearly mandatory. You can't fish a small fly successfully on a heavy leader and you can't, in turn, keep from breaking a fine leader with

a stiff, heavy rod. As a result, fly tackle is the most refined, most worried-over tackle in the world and because of its delicacy it is the least fatiguing to the angler and the most sporting in terms of magnifying the fish.

For example, I once killed a salmon of over twenty pounds on a small #10 wet fly. I had first rolled him on a sensible #6 and then gone to a #8, but under those low-water conditions he preferred to wait for the #10 before fastening firmly. Actually, I deserved to lose that fish because I choked and played him far too lightly and too long, but my point still stands. That's an awfully large fish to hook on a fly about a half-inch long.

Similarly, I once hooked a trout of between eight and ten pounds on a tiny #18 dry fly, and this was no fluke, either. I had seen him rising steadily to small naturals in the clear water and he wouldn't take till I gave him the correct color and size. In this case, however, I was robbed. I'm still convinced I deserved to land that fish, as I very nearly did, but that's a story in itself.

Nearly as important, it seems to me, is the fact that these fish live and feed in relatively shallow running water most of the time. The joy of small lures and light tackle would be canceled out if these fish hid themselves in the depths. The fight would bog down, and you certainly wouldn't dare use that three-ounce rod if your flies had to be lowered a hundred feet or more on metal line or with a sinker the size of a sash-weight. Then, too, you would miss the thrill of seeing the fish take as you usually do when fishing shallow runs and flats.

Another seldom-mentioned blessing of this type of fishing is that the game is usually played alone and on foot. The law may state that nonresidents must hire a guide for salmon fishing in Canada, but this is more a local employment scheme than a necessity. And, even though a few very large rivers are more easily fished from a boat for both salmon and trout, this is the exception rather than the rule. This ability to fish effectively without guide, crew, boat, outriggers, depth-finders, and other intruding paraphernalia adds greatly to the joy and intimacy of fishing. There's a reward to this sort of one-on-one confrontation that is hard to describe, but veteran surf-casters will understand instinctively. Most of them would rather catch one good fish from the beach than a dozen from a boat. So would that small group of dedicated bonefishermen who prefer to stalk the flats on foot even though they know their chances would be better in a skiff with a good guide.

Certainly, any gamefish deserving a top rating must have strength, style, and heart. The trouts rank very high in all three. Most species are acrobatic performers—salmon and rainbows especially. Yet browns and brooks, especially those in their early prime measuring twelve to eighteen inches, take to the air with surprising regularity when they're in peak condition. Admittedly, no trout will jump as high or as often as a tarpon. None will run as fast or as far as a bonefish. And none may give you the long, dogged, tugging fight of a jack. But even if trout don't win any particular event, they are all-around performers—probably the decathlon champions among fish.

Trout have one enormous energy source that is denied to almost every other freshwater fish: the ability to utilize the boundless pasturages of the oceans. Very few fish can migrate from fresh to salt water and back, but this is precisely what all the trout, including the brook trout, can do. Running water has little or no plankton—a primary food source at the bottom of the chain—and is, therefore, much less productive than still water. To make up for this, these fish will run out to sea, grow at a fantastic rate, and then obligingly deliver themselves back to your doorstep several times as large as they could ever get on river food.

Dams and pollution have cut off so many trout populations from the ocean that it's easy to forget this bonus, but all species will make this migration where and if this opportunity still exists. The mighty steelhead of the Pacific Northwest are only sea-going rainbows. The famous sea trout of Europe are merely sea-run browns. And the "salters" of Cape Cod and the "sea-trout" of Canada's Maritime Provinces are just brookies that have packed on the poundage during a season in the Atlantic.

This type of fishing rewards skill and punishes error because the quarry is shy and feeds selectively. This makes the capture of a trout especially rewarding. Yet if you choose the right fly and present it with delicacy and imagination after a cautious approach, you can succeed with pleasing regularity.

A complete novice might well hook into a near-record bluefish or striper on his first outing in a charter boat, but I'll lay you ten to one he couldn't catch a trout worth keeping his first day astream and he'd be lucky to catch a really decent one in his first full week.

Another amenity of trout fishing is that the fish tend to distribute themselves fairly evenly throughout a river, with every good lie holding at least a fish or two. When you approach a productive-looking pool or run, you can be almost certain trout are there. It's up to you to figure out when, how, and on what they will be feeding. On the other hand, fish that school up make for feast-or-famine fishing—a lucky angler may make a killing by stumbling onto a wandering school while a more skillful one may go blank because the schools decided to avoid him that day.

Best of all, fishing for the trout tends to become a way of life and leads the angler into more related hobbies and interests than any other sport. Certainly trout gear is talked about and tinkered with more than any other type of tackle, but that's just part of the game. I mean full-fledged hobbies in their own right. Fly tying is a notable example. So is rod-building—especially for those few who still experiment with tapers and actions by planing their own raw bamboo. Entomology has been taken up by thousands of enthusiastic fly tyers and fly fishermen. The truly dedicated even get involved in hydrology, geology, chemistry, botany, and the other disciplines that make up ecology in an attempt to understand more about their favorite waters, the life systems they support, and how they can be protected or improved.

Even if you're not an angler, but merely a fish-watcher or fish-eater, you will still be drawn to the trouts. They live in the most beautiful waters of the world—cool, unspoiled streams and rivers. It's true that some mountain lakes are jewels, too, but these are usually trout lakes. Though an increasing number of our waters of all kinds have become soupy and shabby-looking, I have never seen a first-rate salmon or trout river that was not lovely to look at. For when man has butchered the trees the water is no longer cool. Where he has allowed dwellings to clutter and fester, the water is no longer pure. At this point salmon and trout quietly disappear as if they were part of an ethical boycott.

The outward beauty of the trout has been described so often that I need add little here. You may well think this praise has been overdone if you have seen these fish only in restaurant windows or in the baskets of friends who have followed the hatchery truck to your local creek. All these are hatchery fish, raised in sluggish tanks on artificial food, and they are cheap counterfeits, easily detectable on the line, in the hand, or on the table. Then, too, colors of all fish fade soon after they die. To eyewitness these fish in their full splendor you must hold the wild ones in your hands at the moment of capture. Then, to steal a phrase from Izaak Walton, they are "too pleasant to be looked upon, but only on holy-days."

The shape, or conformation, of the trout is another joy to behold. We say pickerel is skinny, a bass is deep, a carp is fat, or a flounder is flat. But compared to what? Compared to a trout, of course. Unconsciously, we take the shape of the trout as the yardstick against which all other fish are measured.

This may be hard to believe, but trout even smell good—at least they do when compared to most other fish. Pike are notoriously slimy and bass have a skin odor that only a fisherman could love—which is why they are usually skinned before cooking. But I have never heard even a fastidious nonfisherman complain about the stench of a fresh-caught trout or salmon. A small point, perhaps, but add it to our total reckoning.

At the risk of being accused of overkill, I must add that the trout are the most obliging of fish even after their capture. They have no sharp spines or fins to puncture the unwary hand. Anyone who has been speared by the tines of a catfish—or even a small bluegill—will appreciate this. Trout lack the deadly dentistry of pike, bluefish, or barracuda, too. And they don't conceal razor blades in their gill-covers as snook do, either.

Trout are pleasingly easy to clean. With pan-sized specimens, merely slit from the vent to the pectoral fins, free the tongue with an outside cut, stick your thumb into this newly created "mouth," and pull downward. One good tug frees tongue, pectoral fins, and guts all of a piece. Now run your thumbnail firmly up the backbone to remove the jellylike kidney and the job is done. No need to scale, skin, or fillet. You can clean four or five trout a minute without hustling in the least. Salmon are even easier to prepare, but we'll take that up later.

The flesh of the trout is the most prized of all fish with fins. Atlantic salmon is selling at over $3.50 a pound right now (ca. 1975) at my fish store—not much below Maine lobster. Trout would probably be equally dear except that wild fish may not be sold in this country and the white-fleshed, pond-reared fish sold to innocents by restaurants and fancy fish stores are as much like wild trout as supermarket chicken parts are like ruffed grouse.

Wild trout as well as salmon have orange or pink flesh when they are in good condition. The trout store up future energy as a pinkish oil that is evenly distributed all through their flesh—a tidier, and certainly tastier, system than larding this surplus on the hips or bellies as do species we all know. This oil is what the salmon lives on during its several-month fast in fresh water; it carries the trout through the rigors of winters, and it makes dining on them both delicious. A spent salmon or a March trout will probably have white flesh—as does the synthetic hatchery model—and is fit only for chowder if you are unwise enough to kill it.

The Atlantic salmon—and the Atlantic salmon alone—goes even further to ingratiate himself to the angler. He delivers himself back from the ocean not only large, lively, and delicious, but with a built-in handle. His caudal, or tail, fin is so stiff when he is mature that you can grab the exhausted fish by the wrist of his tail, lifting him firmly and safely from the water at the moment of truth without the aid of a cumbersome net or disfiguring gaff.

And, as if that were not the peak of accommodation, he also has packaged himself as a hermetically sealed food container. To prepare a salmon for travel or storage, all you do is cut out the gills. There's no need to gut a salmon till you're ready to cook it and, in fact, it keeps better whole. Digestive juices stop flowing once a salmon enters fresh water, so the fish won't eat through its own belly while lying on the ice as other fish surely will. Then, too, bacteria which cause deterioration have a hard time entering the atrophied throat or penetrating the tough skin. I have kicked sawdust off summer salmon that have been lying in an icehouse for six weeks or more and found them every bit as firm and good as the day they were landed. Try keeping any other fish a mere six days, ungutted, and you'll appreciate this trait of the salmon all the more.

And that pretty much winds up my case for the trout. History is witness to the fact these fish have dominated sporting literature, art, and husbandry. The qualities that have raised them to this pre-eminence are the following: they take small food and lures; they live in shallow, intimate waters; they can be caught alone and on foot; they are superb fighters; they grow large at sea and then return to their freshwater home; they reward the skillful and escape the bungler; they spread out over the river in predictable lies, thus reducing the element of pure chance; their pursuit leads into other fascinating hobbies and studies; they take the angler to the most scenic waters; they are beautiful themselves in both color and shape; they are safe to handle, relatively pleasant to smell, easy to clean, and delicious to eat.

That's a staggering list of virtues, isn't it? I can't think of another fish, or group of related fish, that rates half as well in even half these categories.

But don't these fish have at least one fatal flaw? Isn't there some skeleton in the *Salmo* family closet that I am hiding from you? Yes, I'm sorry to say, there is. Salmon are too scarce and most trout are too small—a condition that has been with us for many decades.

Nearly a hundred years ago, the Reverend Myron W. Reed was lamenting, "This is the last generation of trout-fishers. The children will not be able to find any." He was very nearly right, but his timetable was a bit off. He couldn't know that the durable and elusive European brown trout was about to be introduced into our depleted Eastern waters or that the American angler would soon have automobiles and aircraft to carry him to the untapped fisheries of our own West, Canada, and Alaska. The good minister was probably spoiled, anyway. Most of us today would drool at the quality of fishing he was saying the last rites over.

But the facts remain: Our present-day trout are often pitifully small. The average fish taken is probably under ten inches long, but this is the fault of overfishing, not of the fish. Just look at the sizes these fish can attain when given a decent chance. The record brook trout is $11^{1}/_{2}$ pounds—almost exactly the same size as the record smallmouth bass. The record rainbow (51 pounds), cutthroat (41 pounds), and brown trout ($39^{1}/_{2}$ pounds) are nearly twice the size of the biggest largemouth ever landed. And the heaviest rod-caught Atlantic salmon (74 pounds) tops the biggest muskellunge, the species usually considered the largest of all freshwater gamefish.

I can't think of anything more to say in behalf of the trout, unless it's this paraphrase of the famous saying by the Elizabethan physician William Butler: "Doubtless God could have made a better fish. But doubtless God never did."

1975

2

When Trout Feed and Why

When do you mow the lawn and when should you fish? A glance at the sky and at your stream thermometer will tell you.

There is a lot of truth in the old saying that the best time to go fishing is whenever you can get away. Removal of storm windows, mowing of lawns, taxi service to the Cub Scouts, and the like make mighty contributions to the cause of conservation each year.

Yet there are some days, and even some hours of these days, that offer better fishing than others. And the angler who knows when these periods will occur has a greater chance at success because he'll know when it will pay to defer chores, defect, or downright desert. He can be sure the penalties will be worth the crime because he'll be astream when the trout "are really on."

I began to learn how to predict heavy trout-feeding periods purely by accident over twenty years ago when I was made unofficial (and unpaid) manager of a small, northeastern fishery—about a mile of freestone river that averaged forty to fifty feet wide and contained wild brook and brown trout. The water was slightly acidic, therefore not very fertile, and by mid-June the hatches became skimpy at best, and those were few and far between.

It was decided that since stocked fish were expensive and added little to the fishery in the long run, the meager available funds would be used to improve the existing wild population. This meant habitat improvement to create more holding water and supplemental feeding to increase growth, keep resident fish in place, and perhaps encourage some recruiting from downstream.

We bought bags of floating pellets and cast the contents upon the waters liberally and frequently, but the pellets just floated merrily down the stream, untouched by trout. This puzzled me, because a couple of miles downriver, on a heavily stocked section, the trout boiled for the very same brand. It slowly dawned on me that wild trout, as opposed to hatchery stock, wouldn't eat pellets. They hadn't been trained to do so from infancy, and the little brown cylinders didn't look or act anything like their natural insect food.

I was about to scratch the feeding program when I remembered that the famous fly fisher and early twentieth-century stream conservationist Edward R. Hewitt had fed his stream fish with ground beef lungs, or "lights," and he claimed that his wild fish gobbled them up. So I bought some lungs from a small, nearby abattoir, had my local butcher run them through his grinder, and embarked on "Operation Lungburger."

Ground lungs look much like hamburger—a bit paler and pinker, perhaps—and wild trout think they're the greatest thing this side of McDonalds. Equally important, lung tissue floats. What isn't eaten in the first pool floats down below to the next batch of trout, thus cutting down on waste. And, since most of the little pink blobs stay on the surface, you can easily observe the intensity of feeding activity because the fish must break the surface to get the food.

I quickly noticed that sometimes only a few fish would feed, halfheartedly, while at other times the entire pool would erupt for minutes. Same pool. Same trout. Same amount of food. Why the big difference?

Within a few months, I learned how to predict when the fish would feast and when they would fast, and that saved a lot of wasted lungburger—and money. In the early spring and again in fall, trout fed best on sunny days between 1 P.M. and 4 P.M. In bright, mid-summer weather, they fed most actively from 11 A.M. to 12:30 P.M. and in the evening from 7 P.M. until dark. On cloudy days, feeding was mediocre at best at all times of year.

So far I had merely rediscovered the obvious: Trout take natural flies, artificials, and, of course, lungburger far more eagerly under certain fairly predictable conditions than they do under other conditions. But why? What did the excellent feeding times, which varied considerably with the weather and time of year, all have in common?

Temperature offered a tempting lead. I'd noticed that trout didn't start to surface feed on spring days until the water reached 45 degrees Fahrenheit and that they shut down almost completely in summer when it hit 72 degrees. Another clue was the biologists' finding that trout metabolism (their efficiency in using oxygen and digesting food) peaked at about 63 degrees.

From this small start, I soon became a temperature addict. I would dunk my stream thermometer many times each day and jot down the readings along with hour, water level, and weather conditions. I discovered that trout in a small freestone river live on a thermal rollercoaster. On a crisp, sunny day when the water flowed at summer levels, the temperature might be as low as 54 degrees in the early morning and climb to 70 or even 72 degrees by mid-afternoon. That's a 16- to 18-degree difference in a twelve-hour period.

I also noticed that the best dry-fly fishing and feeding periods occurred on just such days—in the morning when water temperatures raced toward, and passed through, the magic 63-degree mark and again at dusk when readings dropped toward that optimum number. In spring and fall, the trout fed best as the temperature climbed past 45 degrees toward 63 degrees—though it seldom reached that high—and feeding ended abruptly when the temperature dropped lower in the late afternoon.

My rule on trout feeding activity on any freestone river—with only two parenthetical qualifiers—can be stated fairly simply: *Trout feed actively when the water temperature (once it has passed 45 degrees or fallen below 72) changes toward 63 degrees, and the faster this rate of change (for that particular river) and the closer it gets to 63, the more active the feeding will be.* I have found no exceptions to disprove this rule in over twenty years of feeding wild trout. However, it is foolproof *only* on freestoners.

On limestone streams, spring creeks, chalkstreams, or on cool flows below dams, temperatures are much less volatile and hourly readings may show little variation. Yet trout on these types of streams snap on and off the feed as quickly as they do on freestoners. So it appears that while a swing in water temperature was a useful indicator of trout activity, it wasn't, perhaps, the sole *cause* of trout-feeding periods. It might be merely the finger that pulled a distinctly different trigger.

Oxygen seemed a likely element to look into, since it takes oxygen to run muscles, digest food, and put on growth. With the possible exception of food, it is the single most important requirement for trout existence. Trout can live for months without food. They die in minutes without oxygen.

My first glance at oxygen as the prime mover looked unpromising. Water at 45 degrees, where trout feeding barely begins, contains over 25 percent more oxygen than water at the trout's optimum 63 degrees. When the temperature rises during a spring noontime or during a late summer morning (and when the fishing should be excellent), the water is actually losing oxygen.

I began searching learned pamphlets and scientific journals for another factor, and I finally found it: *trout metabolism*. This, as I've mentioned, is a measure of the fish's efficiency in digesting food and of its capacity to extract and use oxygen.

I found from one lengthy document that, at top efficiency (presumably 63 degrees), trout can extract *90 percent of the dissolved oxygen from the water* that passes through their gill covers. This makes the gill an extremely effective organ. Our lungs take out only about 25 percent of the oxygen from a lungful of air.

This same monograph told me that gill efficiency varied widely at different temperatures. At both 45 and 72 degrees (where trout feeding usually starts and stops) gill efficiency drops down to about 45 percent or only half of what it is at 63 degrees.

So what is actually happening to the trout when stream temperatures are zooming up to nearly 63 degrees and, in the evening, when they tumble back toward that mark? They are getting extra shots of oxygen into their bloodstreams due to the rapid increase in gill efficiency regardless of how much is dissolved in the stream water. And it is this extra dosage that enlivens the fish and stimulates them to actively search for food—whether or not a hatch of flies is on the water.

Similarly, in spring and fall, when temperatures climb up into the 50s, their gill efficiency is again on the rise and pumping extra oxygen into their blood.

Two added factors make the water contain even more oxygen as the temperature rises from 57 to 64 degrees. One is that warming *water sloughs off oxygen so slowly* that it is often super-saturated or contains more oxygen than the table shows for that temperature. Also, water weeds, diatoms, and algae on the stream bottom are, by photosynthesis, pumping even more dissolved oxygen into the water and further saturating it. As a result, that 7-percent figure could be nearer to 15 percent during this prime feeding period.

However, during the two hours from 12:30 P.M. to 2:30 P.M., as the temperature climbs from 64 degrees to 67.8 degrees (when fishing and feeding are usually poor), there is, by the same means of calculation, a 22-percent *decline* in the trout's blood oxygen. Oxygen intake continues to drop or remain relatively flat during the rest of the afternoon until we get to the 6:30 P.M. to 8:30 P.M. period, when the oxygen intake shows an *increase* of 22 percent. (Actually, the figure is probably slightly lower than this, because cooling water can't take on dissolved oxygen as rapidly. Still, the surge in bloodstream oxygen is impressive.) This may explain why fishing at dusk in summer is so productive.

During spring and fall days, the only period when trout are receiving an extra shot of oxygen is from about 12:30 P.M. to 3 P.M.

For some inscrutable reason best known to the trout, total oxygen intake is *not* the cause of trout-feeding activity. It is the sudden increase (after certain temperature requirements have been met) that spurs this activity. For example, on cloudy summer days, when the water temperature hovers around the perfect 63 degrees all day long and the trout are getting a steady, maximum supply of oxygen, fishing results and response to batches of lights are uniformly mediocre at all times of day.

It may seem that I have complicated things unnecessarily by going into the oxygen-intake theory when the simple temperature readings alone can tip you off on any freestoner. But for those fortunate few who fish limestoners, spring creeks, and the like and where changes in flow and temperature are often barely detectable, it is a necessary second step. Such streams are usually paved with water weed. Bright sunshine can cause the vegetation to pump extra oxygen into the water, making the trout come on the feed suddenly and heavily—even though your thermometer registers little or no change.

It is also interesting to note that there is strong evidence that most (though certainly not all) aquatic insects seem to hatch under similar conditions and in response to the same stimuli. But that's only logical. The genetic strains of wild trout that have survived and reproduced would be precisely the ones best tuned in to their prey's time of greatest availability and vulnerability.

M.C. WEILER

So, after twenty years of observing trout-feeding patterns under relatively controlled conditions, my advice is as follows. Avoid rainy, cloudy days if you have any reasonable choice. Contrary to the old wisdom, they offer poor fishing. Also, don't consult any of the charts or tables that promise to show good feeding days or hours from a year in advance. They are no better than throwing a dart at the calendar. And don't feel that because the fish haven't been feeding well for two days they must be starving. Trout can go for months without food and show no signs of discomfort or agitation. They probably won't feed well on the following day either, unless the weather changes for the better.

Do, however, try to take advantage of the sunny, high-barometer days. And do dip your thermometer regularly to get to know your home river's prime fishing hours, and then make the most of them.

I'll admit that an expert upstream nympher can almost always catch some fish under the worst of conditions. After all, a trout will take a weighted nymph (or a worm, for that matter) if it threatens to bump him on the nose—even though this is more self-defense than actual feeding. However, I find this sort of fishing extremely hard work that demands excruciating concentration. I have more fun and catch far more trout when they're willing to come up off the bottom and take a fly with relish and confidence.

If you watch the weather and your thermometer carefully and fish when the trout are most likely to feed, you'll come to expect better fishing—*if* you don't let minor duties and obligations interfere with something as crucial as your trout fishing.

1988

3

Trout-Taking Places

"Reading a stream" is fine
as far as it goes.
But trout also hang out
in a lot of seldom-fished places.

For many years my knowledge of trout lies was gathered by two simple methods. In some cases I actually saw a fish as it scurried away for cover ahead of me. At other times I located their positions from the rise-forms they made on the surface. The latter observations were usually the most useful, but I have since discovered that these sightings can be misleading.

Fish actively feeding will often be drawn a long way from their holding positions by an abundance of a certain type of food in a particular area. This is especially true of trout that inhabit pools. For instance, fish feeding on emerging duns at the head of a pool in the early afternoon may well be the same ones you saw the evening before at the very tail of the pool while they were sipping spinners 100 or 200 yards downstream.

I discovered this the hard way many years ago after I had raised and pricked a large trout at the tail of a long pool just as darkness fell. I went back for that particular prize mornings and evenings for several days and yet I never saw the fish in that location again. What I didn't realize till then was that this fish had his resting lie farther up the pool and had drifted downstream on that particular evening under an especially generous supply of spent flies.

Since then I have added two more methods to my trout-locating repertory. This new research has changed a lot of my previous ideas about where the majority of the trout spend most of their time. I have discovered that the places where they are caught—riffles, runs, pockets, and heads of pools—are not necessarily the areas of densest trout population. They are merely the places where the ruffled water surface makes it easier for fly fishermen to fool any fish that happen to be there.

Of course, any discussion of trout lies should be prefaced by a description of the habits of the various species of trout. Rainbow trout are far fonder of fast water than are brooks and browns. They prefer deep, rapid runs and are sometimes caught in rushing white water where a brown-trout fisherman would never bother to make a cast. Most brook trout, on the other hand, will choose lies in the slower, more exposed parts of the stream. Perhaps this is due to the fact that larger, more aggressive brown trout often chase them out of the choicest lies. I know of one river that contains all three species, and the way they sort themselves out into different water types provides a vivid example of their different water preferences. Brown trout seem to choose water that is slower than the rainbow's favorite lies, but faster than the currents usually selected by brook trout. Most of the observations in this chapter deal with waters containing either brown trout exclusively or a mixture of brown and brook trout.

A few years ago when I began feeding the wild trout in a small river a supplementary diet of floating lights, some of my previous ideas about trout positions were shaken. I soon noticed that fish rose to this ground meat in good numbers all the way down the pool and that there seemed to be no concentration of trout at the head where the current poured in—even though this was the place where most of the fish were being caught. As this distribution of

trout seemed to be the rule in nearly all the pools and long flats where I fed, I decided to check and make sure that the fish were truly residents of the parts of the pool where they appeared and were not merely following the food down from the riffle at the head.

I chose a sunny, windless midmorning when visibility would be at its best for my next experiment. I crept up a steep bank overlooking a good pool and started observing the water below. I was positioned about two-thirds of the way down the pool where the current flowed slowly at a depth of three to four feet. With the sun high and slightly behind me. I didn't even need polaroid glasses to make out the small pebbles and caddis cases lying on the bottom.

I soon picked out several suckers and then I saw a small trout, much better camouflaged, hovering in midcurrent. For fifteen minutes I observed, taking an informal trout census of the area under clear view, a patch of about fifty feet by thirty. I counted six trout in all, four in the five- to six-inch range and two in the eight- to nine-inch category as well as four much larger chubs. Frankly, I was disappointed with this meager inventory, but the game wasn't over yet.

A shout to my accomplice 150 yards upriver was the pre-arranged signal for him to start tossing handfuls of ground lights into the riffle above, spreading the food generously across the width of the stream. I soon heard the plops of feeding trout upriver, but it seemed nearly two minutes before the first red specks of lights floated into view.

I had no idea, before this, what two pounds of lights looked like as it floated down a pool. It may not seem like much in bulk or weight when you carry it to the river, but once it churns through a rapids and separates into individual particles it seems literally to blanket the water. I peered intently at my chosen patch of river as the red tide of this instant hatch began to cover the surface below me. A small trout blipped to the surface and streaked down warily toward the bottom. Then, another made a darting rise and, in a matter of a few seconds, all the trout and the chubs I had marked down before were rising confidently and regularly.

Suddenly I noticed a much better trout, a twelve-incher, feeding with the others. Where had he come from? If he'd drifted downstream with the artificial hatch, I'm sure I would have seen him earlier. I looked up-current for approaching fish, but saw none. Then, when I turned my attention back to my chosen sector of water, there were four good fish feeding—no, there were five and all ran between eleven and fourteen inches.

And this is the way a good hatch works. A trout river seems to operate on the same principle as a henyard: Once a few fish start feeding the others join in, even though they may be crammed full of food. With trout, though, the smaller fish always start feeding first, and the larger are only pulled to the surface after the hatch and the rising has proceeded for a considerable length of time. Perhaps this is why truly large trout rise toward the end of a two- or three-hour hatch while a half-hour flurry, no matter how intense, seldom affects the sixteen-inch-and-over class of trout.

The trail of lights was thinning out now so I decided to concentrate on one sizable trout and follow his course back to his mysterious lie. This fish soon stopped surface feeding since the trail of lights had now passed on down-current, yet he hovered at mid-depth with his fins quivering—obviously on the lookout for another gift of manna from above. I kept my full attention on this one fish for five or ten minutes and then curiosity got the better of me. I stole a quick glance downstream to see if the other trout I'd observed were still in their feeding stations and, when I turned back to my original subject, he had disappeared.

I have since repeated this experiment several times in an attempt to find out where these trout come from and disappear to, but in every case the trout have just faded away or my attention span has been broken before I could track a good trout back to his holding lie. There was no indication, though, that the trout had moved off to another part of the pool. They seemed to melt into the stream bottom, and I suspected that they slid under flat rocks or edged up under the undercut sides of boulders.

The only way to check out this hypothesis was to explore the river with mask and snorkel. This is chilly work because the river in question rarely gets to a comfortable 70 degrees. But I chose a hot afternoon and launched myself at the head of this long pool and started to coast quietly downstream with the gentle current. For the first time, I was getting a true picture of the trout's world. The rocks and depressions in the river bottom stood out clearly as hiding or resting places. The undersurface of the water's skin was a silvery sheet that undulated gently and seemed to press down heavily on the main body of water. The whole effect was that water is more like gelatin than a liquid.

Another surprising thing was the way trout accepted my presence in their element. I could drift within four or five feet of them in most cases before they veered to one side of me, showing more suspicion than alarm. Perhaps they mistook me for a log drifting down-current. In any event, I was no longer the object of terror I was when I appeared upright, wading near the shore.

I began to search for possible hiding spots, submerging for a closer look when I found large flat rocks or interesting undercuts. Once in a while this close approach would send a good trout scurrying, but I didn't find nearly enough of them to explain the total population I had estimated from my lights-feeding experiments. Since that day, I have repeated this bone-chilling exploration many times with the same results: I can't find more than a quarter of the fish I know to be in the pool no matter how carefully I poke and peer into nooks and crannies. And yet, I think the census I take when feeding lights gives the accurate picture of the pool population and its distribution. Perhaps, when I buy a wetsuit and explore during less comfortable times of day, I'll solve this mystery.

One thing I have learned from my underwater fish counting is that the larger trout do not always inhabit the deepest water. I have explored many pools that are eight to ten feet deep only to discover that the biggest trout in the pool—a solitary old cannibal—has his hiding place in a scant two or three feet of water. A large trout appears in the same lie, year after year near the shallow tail end of a very deep pool. He lies under a great slab of rock not two feet below the surface and fades slowly back into his cavernous retreat whenever I approach. Apparently, it is the degree of protection and possibilities of even further retreat that attract the larger fish rather than depth of water. Unfortunately, such specimen fish seldom engage the dry-fly angler—unless he's willing to go out at midnight.

Trout seem to have a strong preference for certain types of bottom cover against which they appear to be more difficult to detect. They won't lie over a sandy bottom if there is rock, coarse gravel, or rubble nearby. Similarly, they avoid lying over a continuous sheet of ledge rock. I know several places where current concentration and depth are ideal for brown trout and yet I never take a fish there because the bottom, at that point, is smooth rock. Trout seem to feel vulnerable over a monotone background and will avoid holding there if any other alternative presents itself.

Patches of freshly disturbed rock or gravel are seldom attractive to trout but for quite another reason. Until rocks grow a soothing layer of algae they probably feel like sandpaper to the soft underbelly of the fish. This fact may save billions of trout eggs from destruction every year. I have noticed that when trout are spawning during a spell of exceptionally high water they will always make their redds over the slippery stones that have been covered even during low water. They are not tempted to dig out the abrasive stones in the stream margin where their eggs would soon be left high and dry.

My experiments with lights and snorkeling have yielded two bits of information that have helped me locate good trout lies even on strange water. The first is that trout choose their holding spots according to a strict set of priorities. First of all comes safety. Trout will put up with a lot of inconvenience to possess an attack-proof sanctuary, and the most secure lies will usually hide the best fish. Comfort is the next consideration. Trout won't take up residence where the current is exhaustingly strong or where the bottom is not to their liking. Last of all comes the availability of food. Fish are willing to travel quite a distance to the food-bearing current as long as they are secure and comfortable during their resting hours.

The other thing I have learned is that pools and especially long, deep flats hold far more trout than fishing results would indicate. This knowledge has allowed me to enjoy more productive fishing hours per day—or per season—than ever before.

1973

4

Brookies in the Briny

Is there a large, untapped pool
of wild, sea-dwelling brook trout off
our Maine and Canadian coasts?

These days wild brook trout fishing is pretty much confined to cold, headwater brooks and to remote wilderness areas. Yet in Colonial days, brookies were not only abundant, but they were also nearly ubiquitous in the northeastern United States and in Canada from Ontario eastward. At one time, all the deep or cool enough ponds, lakes, and streams in that vast area teemed with natives. That, of course, was before we nearly fished them out, then unwittingly guaranteed their near-extinction in many still waters by stocking the waters with dominant bass. And, until we deforested, overheated, dammed, and polluted our coastal streams and rivers, vast numbers of brook trout fattened up at sea like salmon then ran upriver in April and May for summer residency and fall spawning. These were the "silver trout" of Long Island (almost extinct), the "salters" of Cape Cod (now rare), and the "sea trout" of Maine and the Canadian Maritimes (fortunately still numerous in a few northern rivers).

Yet just possibly, there are still large populations of brook trout that have escaped discovery and exploitation. These are little-known strains that apparently have even saltier tastes than "sea trout" and reside primarily in the ocean. Once, several years ago, I ran across a huge shoal of such brookies that should have been called "oceanies." These fish seemed to prefer the sea as a regular home and to spend the minimum amount of time in fresh water for spawning and infancy.

My discovery of this group of fish was a pure accident because, at the time, brook trout couldn't have interested me less. Six of us had flown into the lower reaches of Labrador's Eagle River by float plane to fish for Atlantic salmon during the first week in July. While we were still standing on the pontoons, unloading, the head guide gave us the bad news. The season was very late. There were still several miles of shelf ice clinging to the coast. No salmon had entered the river. In other words, we should have been there next week.

The first day's fishing proved how right he was. We casted our hearts out and our arms off over the best pools and choicest lies and nobody had so much as a tug or a boil. That evening at dinner, the party leader, who was already catching some thinly disguised abuse, tried to offer an alternative activity: "Why don't we all go to the big city tomorrow and see the sights?"

When the snarling died down, he explained, "We can pack picnic lunches and motor down the bay to Cartwright. It's only two, maybe three, hours by boat. Anyway, it's something to do," he added lamely.

And that's what we did. With two of us to each outboard-powered twelve-footer, we slalomed through the boulders down the lower river and out onto the open bay below, heading for Cartwright, some thirty miles away. We jarred our teeth and jammed our spines pounding over the waves, putting up flights of puffins and sea ducks, and outrunning several seals and porpoises until we finally reached the Metropolis of the North. This consisted of a two-man Mountie barracks, a small Hudson's Bay store, a slightly larger Grenfell Mission that doubled as a school in season, and a handful of small houses.

Since there were no movies or television, few books, and very little retail trade, conversation was the major sport, hobby, and full-time industry of Cartwright. We quickly learned that a shortwave radio report that morning said that the first salmon had been caught at Battle Harbour, some 100 miles to the south, which meant that fish should be in the Eagle within two days. (This bit of intelligence proved to be right on the money and we had indecently good salmon fishing during the last four days of our week, but that, as they say, is another parable.)

After this good news had been thoroughly discussed, we went on to such trivia as last winter's snowfall and minimum temperature, whether or not the shelf-ice was breaking up, the types of seabirds and sea-mammals we'd seen on our trip, and finally to the pack of wolves we had noticed on a small, barren island out in the bay.

That drew a laugh. "Those aren't wolves. They're our sled dogs."

Then why were they doing time on Devil's Island?

"Well, they're no use to us in summer, now are they? Besides, they're liable to chew up some small kids in the village."

What do they find to eat out there?

"Nothing. We have to go out every couple of days and throw them some fish."

Oh? What kind of fish?

"Mostly cod. We jig for them right out front here. But if the cod move out, as they do sometimes, we have to run all the way across the bay and catch trout for them under those cliffs over there."

Were there trout there now?

"They're always there, spring, summer, fall. In winter you just chop a hole in the ice and load up a sledfull."

Fortunately, some of us had lugged along rods and vests in case we ran across a tempting brook emptying into the bay. With several hours to kill and stimulating topics of conversation dwindling, two boatloads of us headed for the cliffs, clearly visible in the distance.

We dropped anchors some seventy feet offshore in six or eight feet of water, as advised, and surveyed our surroundings. Shoreline rocks were blanketed with seaweed. Licked test-fingers confirmed that the water was as salty as it gets this side of Utah. We were thirty miles from the nearest freshwater influence and the headland in front of us showed no "V" hinting at an underground brook or large spring welling up out of the ocean floor. It looked about as trouty as Lower New York Harbour.

We all agreed that we were probably victims of some far-north version of the classic snipe-hunt, but we decided that, when on a fool's errand, do as fools do. We all knotted on streamer flies and went through the motions of casting. Within seconds, all four of us were playing sizable fish.

The first specimens boated puzzled us for a moment. They appeared bright silver with the sunlight reflecting off them, but, when tilted slightly to reduce the glare, the telltale spots on their sides and worm-markings on their backs could be made out faintly. And, of course, the black-and-white edgings on the lower-body fins were a dead giveaway. They were bona fide Eastern Brook Trout, all right, despite their shiny suits.

They acted like typical, freshwater brookies, too. They put up a strong, stubborn fight, boring for bottom, rarely making a sur-

face swirl, much less a jump. And they had that maddening, brook-trout second wind, bolting off at the last moment just when you thought you had them whipped, belly-up.

None of them could be classified as monsters, yet none were minnows, either. The smallest ran about fourteen inches and a very few topped eighteen. All were trim and elegantly proportioned. There wasn't a "Footballer" in the lot. Apparently, they converted the lush sea diet into length as well as girth and they appeared to be young, fast-growing fish. Even the largest males lacked the exaggerated jaws you usually find on a grandfather brookie.

It was the nearest thing to fishing in a hatchery pond I've ever experienced in the wild. If your fly didn't snag up on a piece of floating seaweed, it was nearly impossible to retrieve a forty-foot cast without hooking a fish and if that one wriggled off, another would have it before you could get in enough line to recast. We moved the boats from time to time, a couple of hundred feet this way and that, yet results never changed. That entire area was paved with trout—dozens and dozens of acres of them.

I have never before or since wearied of catching too many one-to three-pound brook trout, but a half hour of this began to pall so I decided to experiment. I tied on a size #12, muskrat-fur nymph and pitched that out. Trout gobbled it up as eagerly as they had the big, gaudy streamer. "O.K.," I muttered, "you might have mistaken that for a small shrimp, but I'll bet you've never seen anything like this out here." I knotted on a well-greased, size #10 March Brown Variant. On the very first cast, that high-floater was sucked under by a two-pounder in a style that would have done a Beaverkill brown proud. And I continued to catch fish after fish on that driest of flies until it got so bedraggled it wouldn't float anymore.

An hour and a half of such fish-hauling was all a grown man could stand, so we headed back to Cartwright to gas up, join up, and pound our way back to camp. But looking back on that once-in-a-lifetime experience now, some tantalizing questions come to mind.

What did those fish feed on? Probably small shrimp and capelin—a smeltlike fish that tries to overpopulate the North Atlantic. I don't know for sure. We kept no fish so we never examined stomach contents. But one thing is certain: They weren't living off March Brown duns even though, for some inscrutable reason, they relished the floating imitation I offered them.

How much—or how little—time did they spend in streams or rivers? It's virtually certain they were born and raised in fresh water. Yet the Hudson's Bay men said they sometimes caught five- to six-inch babies out there and that the fish seemed every bit as plentiful in September and October when they should have been upriver spawning.

But now to the most intriguing question of all: Are northern, sea-dwelling brook trout limited to that one location? It seems doubtful, but I've never revisited Cartwright to explore the possibilities. Were there other concentrations of "oceanies" in other, unfished parts of that large bay? What about the rest of the coves, estuaries, and bays along the indented, Labrador coast? Or along the shores of Newfoundland or Nova Scotia, for that matter? Local cod-fishermen with large baits and hooks might never hook a trout no matter how many of them they were fishing over.

It seems probable that the largest remaining wild brook trout population in the world—with fish averaging two pounds or better—is lying off the coast of northeastern North America just waiting to be discovered by trout fishermen. Any volunteers?

1986

5
A Dirge for Opening Day

Feel that our trout are too few,
too small, too tame?
Count your blessings.

By opening New York State's trout season on April Fool's Day, the powers that be may be trying to tell us something. I can count on the toes of one foot the number of April firsts that have been warm and sunny. Usually, there's a rim of ice along the shore, and we have to trudge through the snow to reach the stream.

Yet fish we will—the hundreds of thousands of us who are suffering from withdrawal symptoms. Not that we expect classic fly fishing. We know we won't see trout sip mayflies from the water surface for weeks to come. But we are emerging from a mandated cold-turkey period of 183—count 'em, 183—trout-fishingless days, and that, in the words of John O'Hara's Pal Joey, is "a long time between drinks."

This year, the day falls on a Friday—a work day. But not to worry. Medical science will be blind-sided by an epidemic of the "salmo" strain of the flu. Only in Vermont has this disease been diagnosed. There, they close schools on opening day in craven surrender to certain truancy.

This Friday will certainly not offer the sort of wilderness experience that would make Thoreau drool. True anglers, tuned in to nature's subtle secrets, will be lined up in neomilitary ranks near bridges and parking areas. Some atavistic instinct tells nature's noblemen that easy-access areas are where the state's trucks have unloaded their tankfuls of hatchery trout.

These recent parolees will huddle, quivering in the near-freezing water, waiting in vain for that manna of pellets from above—the only food they've ever seen since they emerged from their eggs fifteen months before.

And, wonders of all, you will see, in Saturday's and Sunday's newspapers, photos of grinning anglers holding up huge trout with spots on their sides as big as dimes. Yes, Virginia, there are still big, wild trout in our nearby streams and rivers. But in nothing like the numbers that flourished only a few decades ago.

I have yet to be fitted for a wheelchair, yet I can remember the days when I could count on having a pool on the main stem of the Beaverkill all to myself. Yes, even on weekends during the peak of spring fishing.

I can't keep from wondering what effect this growing army of trouters is having on our streams as self-sustaining natural resources. I have recently seen rich limestone streams in central Pennsylvania that have been scuffed down to bare stones. Only a few years back, they were noted for their forests of waving water weeds—havens for millions of scuds, shrimp, and insect larvae that are the essential foods of wild trout. Today, stream traffic is so heavy that the moment a tendril pokes up between the pebbles, it is crunched off by a felt-soled wading shoe.

Then there's famous Silver Creek in Idaho. It is so steadily trampled that state authorities are considering limiting the number of anglers per day to protect the stream bottom. What about our even more pressured eastern streams? Already you have to reserve your four-hour slot on Long Island's Connetquot. How long before we have to draw lots, the way western hunters do for elk permits, for some footage on the Amawalk? Is there any way to prevent trout fishing from sinking to the level of an amusement park concession?

But these are dark thoughts for such a hope-filled time of year. After all, there are a full six months of trout season ahead of us. And I clearly recall exhilarating words from some old book: "For, lo, the winter is past, and the voice of the trout is heard in our land"—though I may have a word or two wrong, there.

I am absolutely certain, though, that years from now, our children will be regaling their children with tales of trout rising recklessly as far as the eye could see. They will be casting back to the late 1980s, remembering them as "the good old days." And, do you know what? Maybe they are . . . maybe they are.

1988

6

Great-Grandfather's Trout

What happened to the Northeast's
original glut of wild brook trout?
Blame greed and poor biology.

"**W**ell, you can add another fish to my tally," I said to the guide. "How are you coming along?"

The guide answered with a grunt that told me he was equally disinterested in big numbers and small talk. Still, my count of fifty-seven was impressive whether or not it was precise. For it wasn't a tally of the number of casts I had made nor the number of fish I had raised, but the count of the wild brook trout actually landed and released. That's not bad in this day and age, even if these weren't the giants of Labrador. But they were rock hard, brilliantly painted, and as eager as they were plentiful—averaging nine to ten inches with the occasional bonus fish in the twelve- to fifteen-inch class.

My host, who was working out of the other end of the rowboat, had been equally busy, which meant that in less than three hours we'd caught and released well over a hundred trout. I doubt that we could have scored much better at a hatchery.

"I've never fished a lake this loaded before. Anywhere. Ever," I said. "Can you imagine what it must have been like back a hundred years ago?"

"You know," the guide said, "there's just a chance we can find out. There are some old logbooks back at the lodge that might have some records in them."

We were fishing in one of a group of small lakes and ponds in northern New England that had remained isolated for more than a century. I can't tell you exactly where: I'm under a blood-oath not to reveal the location. And even if I did, the one road into this fishery is both locked and guarded. But, piggy as it may sound, that is the sole reason why the fishing here has held up. All the accessible lakes and ponds for hundreds of miles around had been fished down to mediocrity, or less, before the turn of the century.

After a late evening of fishing and an even later supper, my host pulled a dusty logbook off a high shelf and we started digging. Most of the early entries, dating back to the late 1870s, were flowery and vague. Others focused on moose, deer, ducks, and wildflowers. A few, though, did mention the sizes and numbers of fish taken.

Successful outings listed catches of between fifty and a hundred fish per rod—about what we'd been taking—with the biggest reaching toward 1½ pounds and the odd one stretching to 2. Our best fish that day had measured a bit over fifteen inches, though another angler had reported one of seventeen. It appeared that the fishing hadn't changed that much over the years after all. Because of an unwritten club rule that you killed only what you wanted to eat while you were there (no coolers of iced trout were taken out at the end of your stay), natural production had kept pace with the harvest. Apparently, we were casting our flies into a time capsule. We were privileged to experience a perfectly preserved example of a brief, but little-remembered, chapter in the history of American sport fishing.

Recreational angling—as opposed to fish-gathering—didn't amount to much until after the Civil War. Up to that time, most Americans were too busy fighting Indians, clearing forests, or growing food to indulge in sport for sport's sake. But, starting in the 1860s, cities and factories grew rapidly, wealth accumulated, and the more fortunate beneficiaries of the industrial revolution, like their counterparts in Europe, turned to riding to hounds, wing shooting, and fly fishing.

Trout fishing in eastern America differed in several ways from the sport in Europe, however. The fish itself had stricter living requirements: eastern brook trout needed cooler water than European trout. On top of this, the New England climate lacked the leavening influence of the Gulf Stream and was far hotter in summer. For these reasons our native American trout were confined to cold headwater streams, deep mountain lakes, or far northern latitudes.

Brook trout are also shorter lived than their European cousins. The allotted span for most brookies is three years in running water, though they may stretch that to five or six years in still waters where the living is easier.

The majority of these narrow brooks were hemmed in by trees or bordered by alders that not only made elegant fly casting impossible, but played host to swarms of black flies or mosquitoes during the best angling months. The more open waters of larger streams were usually too warm in summer and were dominated by pickerel, perch, and chubs until the more temperature-tolerant brown trout were transplanted from Europe. No wonder the "sports" of the day took to the high ponds and lakes of the Adirondacks, northern New England, and southern Canada, leaving the nearby mountain brooks to the happy farm boy with hook and worm.

These northern waters not only held larger trout, but were thought to contain a limitless supply of them. Furthermore, still waters offered more comfortable and genteel angling.

Of course, this Eden wasn't without its serpent, and that snake-in-the-grass turned out to be the "gentleman" angler himself. In those days there was little awareness that even in lakes, brook trout were not immune to overfishing. Suntanned men returned from outings lugging crates filled with iced trout as proof of prowess. It took surprisingly few years to deplete these once-bountiful fisheries, and

each season anglers journeyed farther north into New England and Canada, leap-frogging the fished-out waters nearer to home.

These lakes and ponds might have recovered under prudent management and wise regulation, but most never had a chance. One of the first steps taken by the fledgling fishery science of the day was to restock with smallmouth bass from the Mississippi watershed. Smallmouths, it was reasoned, were hardier, more prolific, larger, and could withstand fishing pressure better than brook trout while remaining equally game fighters. All true, but what scientists failed to understand was that any fish that can keep northern pike populations pruned down can virtually eradicate the more vulnerable trout. Not long after the turn of the century, most northeastern lakes had become bass fisheries. The few that were limited to their original populations of trout, and perhaps landlocked salmon, were so highly prized that they were subjected to devastating fishing pressure. By my early childhood back in the 1930s, those great old lakes with the thundering names—Parmachene, Memphrem-agog, Mooslookmeguntic—had already been reduced to lackluster fisheries.

At the same time, developments that were to change the focus of sport fishing were taking place. Split-cane rods, vacuum-dressed silk fly lines, and eyed hooks were all invented during this period. The freer-rising brown trout was being introduced then, too. All these innovations made long, accurate casts and dry-fly fishing on streams not only possible but popular, while they offered few benefits to stillwater anglers.

The lake-fishing technique of the day had been borrowed from a tried-and-true method long used for trout on the highland lochs of Scotland. It consisted of a team of wet flies fished with a long rod and a short, light, level line so that the top dropper fly would skip across the surface on the retrieve.

Limber rods of ten feet or more and light lines were standard lake equipment; no other type of tackle could keep the fly or flies high enough to dip in and out of the surface on the short retrieve. These were certainly miserably balanced outfits for modern fly casting, but they performed their task admirably.

Only in terminal tackle were there any real differences between American and British lake-fishing gear. American flies soon became larger and gaudier because our brook trout seemed to prefer them. And while the British kept their level leaders as light as possible out of respect for the spookier brown trout, Americans tied what looked like hawsers to the ends of their lines. I still have a few old leaders from my grandfather's kit that I keep as curiosities. They're only six feet long, and have loops on both ends as well as two more loops at two-foot intervals for easy attachment of the snelled flies as droppers. The big surprise is that not only were these leaders tied up out of gut heavy enough to kill a salmon, but all strands were doubled for good measure!

Could one still catch trout with such archaic gear? I decided I would try to find out on my third and last day on that unspoiled lake in New England. There were no old-time rods rigged up and

hanging from the walls of the lodge, but I had brought a ten-and-
a-half-foot graphite light-salmon rod that could serve as my long
rod. Though it called for an 8-weight line, I put a 4 on it in an effort
to duplicate the old light lines. Lastly, I tied up
the leader out of double strands of 12-pound-test monofilament
with bulky dropper loops and all. A few practice casts on the lawn
in front of the lodge told me that I had created as miserable a casting machine as human ingenuity could devise.

Out on the lake, I was faced with making a decision on fly patterns. The nearest I could come to the once-popular Scarlet Ibis
was a gaudy Mickey Finn streamer. This went onto the end of the
leader. The Brown Hackle with peacock body and the Montreal that
had once been so popular as duller dropper flies were not to be
found in my fly boxes, so I substituted wet-fly patterns of the March
Brown and Leadwing Coachman as close approximations. And, to
keep the game fair, I attached my droppers to the leader with four
inches of 12-pound monofilament. My host took one look at this
improvised rig and asked whether I was trying for trout or tuna.

A fresh breeze rippled the lake surface that morning. It
improved my chances, but it also destroyed my ability to cast in an
upwind direction. However, I soon found out that I could lob the
flies over thirty feet downwind, and I realized why the old-timers
always advised casting downwind from a drifting boat. There was
nothing else they could possibly do.

While I thrashed from the stern of the boat with streamer fly
and two dancing droppers, my host was casting from the bow, drawing a well-sunk wet fly or streamer with a slow, irregular retrieve
in the present-day manner. Although I didn't keep count (I felt the
guide frowned on this), I had the distinct impression that I was
doing at least as well as, and perhaps a little better than, my host.

The evening fishing—that great hour and a half before dark—
was a different matter, though. The chop had gone from the surface. The lake looked glassy and lead-colored, and I feared that my
stout leader would spook every self-respecting trout in the neigh-
borhood. The gaudy streamer fly at the submerged end of the thick

leader did, indeed, lose much of its appeal under these conditions. But the top dropper, which skipped across the surface several inches below the hard-to-see airborne leader, more than made up the difference. It accounted for some 90 percent of the trout I took that evening.

Presenting the dropper fly on this glassy surface called for a variation in technique from the morning fishing when the wind and waves helped give life to the fly. When drawing a dropper fly over the top of a slick surface, a sideways wobble to the rod tip makes the fly zigzag like an egg-laying caddisfly and greatly increases its effectiveness. This was a technique I had nearly forgotten since it had been shown to me many years ago by an Adirondack guide who had always outfished me.

Toward dark, when the trout could be seen rising all around us, my host switched to a dry fly. It was surprisingly ineffective, and it worked only slightly better when, in frustration, he twitched it to catch the fish's attention.

I'm sorry to say that I landed only about half the fish that whacked my fly solidly that evening. Many that hit hard enough to jolt the rod were off in a flash. I had to conclude that trout that could normally have been hooked firmly were tearing loose on the strike because my modern salmon rod was too stiff and unyielding for this type of fishing. The floppy old fly rods one finds in attics may seem ludicrous for modern stream fishing, but they were tailor-made for early lake angling.

Then too, that stout gut—especially the heavy snells on the dropper flies—wasn't a product of ignorance, either. The very stiffness of the gut made the dropper fly stand out at right angles to the leader and made dancing or zigzagging it over the surface that much easier. In fact, all of the old-timers' tackle—from rod to fly—wasn't as tacky as it appears. When put to the test, great-grandfather's fishing tackle made sense.

Though I've described this type of fishing as exciting, I'll have to admit that it's also easy. Given a few minutes of demonstration and a half-hour's practice, anyone can dance a dropper fly enticingly at that close range. The fish aren't gut-shy or afraid of the boat. During a dusk feeding orgy, trout will swirl to naturals within a few feet of the hull. It is fishing made-to-order for beginners or part-timers.

On unspoiled waters like these, the entire family could pile into boats or canoes after supper and even the young children or non-fishing wives could enjoy catching more than enough trout for breakfast. Boats could stay close together and anglers could chat as they fished without hurting their chances. Compared to the solitary disciplines of stream fishing, this sport was as sociable and forgiving as a friendly game of croquet on the front lawn.

And that, perhaps, is the chief reason why this type of trout fishing left so few traces in angling literature. It was more social than skillful. It had more in common with party-boat fishing than with matching the hatch for wise brown trout in a clear stream. Still, I can't help wishing we had more of these "time capsule" fisheries passed down from great-grandpa's time. For even though you know, deep down, that your skill and knowledge aren't responsible, there's something wonderfully encouraging about catching (and releasing) trout after trout—at least once in a while.

1985

7

More Trout per Mile

Avid birders put up nesting boxes
and feeders. Why shouldn't trouters
do the same?

Trout fishing that lies within day-driving distance of our pop-ulation centers is mostly bad and, let's face it, getting worse. Unfortunately, the situation is much like the weather in Mark Twain's day: everybody talks about it, but nobody does anything about it.

Admittedly, sportsmen's groups, state governments, and private owners pour a lot of hatchery trout into our eastern and even into some western streams. But most of these innocents find few places to hide and have little chance for long-term survival. For example, a lady of my acquaintance who owns a stretch of small stream lost all her spring stocking a few years ago due to a late-May flood. Undaunted, she ordered another batch for the end of June. By this time, the water was catastrophically low and, when the fish were dumped in, she and the hatchery man watched in horror as $500 worth of trout stampeded downstream like a school of bonefish and were never seen again.

Stocked fish may not always be such a sudden and total loss, but it's a dubious policy to try to stockpile trout where they simply don't want to live. Hatchery fish are expensive, too. Perhaps trout-fanciers should take a tip from suburban bird watchers. When the binocular boys want to attract and hold songbirds, they plant protective shrubs or bushes and set out bird houses. Why shouldn't trouters build trout houses on their favorite streams?

For what our rundown running waters really need is not more trout but more trout-holding places. Much has been learned and written about improving the richer, more stately flowing streams of the upper Midwest. Yet the problems of the acid, rocky spate rivers of the East have been largely neglected—despite the fact that these are the very waters that support the most fishermen and the fewest trout per mile.

Our larger streams—those averaging eighty feet or more in width—are able to sustain fair fishing through sheer volume of water and depth even when they are severely damaged. Smaller streams and brooks, however, show the effects of erosion dramatically. And these cooler waters, which start nearer the springs and flow at higher altitudes, are the mainstays of both our summer fishing and our resident watershed trout populations. They, in particular, need all the help they can get. The question is: What sort of help?

The solution lies in finding out what fish-producing characteristics these waters used to have before they were trampled by civilization, and restoring them. When oldtimers tell you about all the big fish they used to catch from your favorite stream, they're not necessarily lying.

Timbering and farming started our streams on their downward path. Thinning, even stripping, our watersheds of trees has caused not only pronounced summer droughts, but destructive floods as well. Perhaps stream beds could have handled this challenge if they had been left intact. But the banks came tumbling down when farmers tried to stretch their acres by removing all of the trees right down to the edge of the stream.

Once the climax trees with their massive root structures were removed, floods began to tear out the margins. If you've ever watched a large tree with its twelve-foot-diameter root structure plow its way down a swollen stream bed, you'll understand why so many riverbanks are now composed of shallow, treeless gravel. After years of this chain-reaction bulldozing and uprooting, most of our running waters are two streams wide and half a stream deep.

When you examine the resulting shallow, unproductive flats (no longer pools) and riffles (no longer runs), the remedy may seem deceptively simple. You'd probably suggest that a dam, which would raise the water level two or three feet, could turn the whole stretch of uninviting flats into an angler's promised land.

But you'd be wrong on four counts. First, effective dams are damnably expensive. In many areas, a Hewitt ramp-dam sixty to eighty feet wide may cost several thousand dollars. Second, dams tend to heat up water, making it intolerable to trout. Third, the large amounts of unstable sand and gravel that litter most streams today will soon fill in your dream pool above the dam, leaving only the limited plunge-pool below for fish holding. And fourth, damming creates slow water, which produces only a tenth as much food per

square foot of bottom as running water does. Eastern spate streams, by their character and chemistry, are food-short to begin with, and we shouldn't reduce their larders even further.

The answer lies not in direct confrontation with the current but in using its sudden, destructive power to heal the stream. As a jujitsu expert converts his opponent's strength to his own advantage, you can make a river's floods serve your purpose. You can, that is, if you make use of the proper techniques.

During the past sixteen summers I have spent at least as much time tinkering with running water as I have fishing it, and over that period I've made all the obvious mistakes. On the other hand, I've had a few heartening successes, and if you think catching a fish on a fly you tied yourself is a thrill, just wait till you take a good trout from a productive spot you've created out of waste water with your own two hands.

I'll discuss several other improvement schemes later on, but first I'd like to describe the most versatile and least expensive stream improvement device I've ever seen. This is the *log cribbing*, and although it's far from new and I certainly didn't invent it, I may have improved it some.

Careful planning and foresight must go into the positioning of these structures. They should be built only on the strong side of the current or at least where they will be nearest to the dominant feed lane. Don't place them over ledge rock—no matter how permanent such a location may appear to be. A cribbing can't possibly scour fish-holding undercuts here and trout don't like to lie over uninterrupted Sheetrock, anyway. Choose a place with a gravel or rubble bottom in a shallow riffle or unproductive flat.

Pivotal to your future success is the embedding of the first log. It must be dug into bank or neighboring gravel deeply enough—two or three feet on tight, tree-lined banks, but up to six or eight feet on unstable, shelving shores—so that high waters can't work in behind it and scour it out. At this stage, a little extra digging is money in the bank; it will help you sleep better later on during those nights when the river is in flood.

Logs should be of hemlock, larch, or cedar—woods that can withstand alternate wetting and drying without rotting. Pine is virtually useless and even the choicest hardwoods will disintegrate in a few seasons if they're not totally submerged all the time. Hemlock is usually easy to get in most parts of the Northeast, and it's light enough to handle. Twenty-foot logs a foot across the butt can be moved short distances by one man with a crowbar or cant hook and are the best, all-around size. Try to select ones that are smooth-trunked and knot-free so that debris won't find a place to hang up. Finally, before you lower the first log into its resting place, slice the trailing end in half and remove the top section for twelve to eighteen inches so that the next log will mortise in smoothly.

Before filling in this trench, cut some willow switches slightly longer than the final depth of burial and poke their butts in as far as possible along both sides of the log. Willows planted in saturated sand or gravel are almost sure to take and, once established, are great insurance against the loss of this key log.

The face of the cribbing formed by this log should be slanted out into the current at an angle of no more than 45 degrees and in some cases as little as 30 degrees, depending on the location. Large cakes of ice or whole trees tend to hang up on structures that confront the floodwaters too directly, while more gradual inclines will shrug off menacing objects, deflecting them harmlessly down current.

Whether you build a simple or complex cribbing will depend on the location you have chosen. Construction principles are essentially the same, but a simple one is sooner completed and may make a better choice for your first efforts. The complex cribbing may scour a home for twice as many trout, but it's effective only in special situations—either at a bend in the river or below a diagonal riffle where the current angles sharply toward one bank. (On a straight stretch, this longer structure would have to jut out perilously far into the river, and the second log, to continue the current deflection, would have to be placed at nearly a right angle to the flow.)

The second log to be placed in a simple cribbing, which forms the lower or downstream arm of this widened A-frame skeleton, should be equally well trenched and anchored into the bank, then mortised and spiked into the first one. To make sure you won't lose your future rock ballast when the cribbing has been deeply undercut by high water, attach heavy-gauge, widemesh (eight-inch or more) wire fencing of four-foot or more width to the inside of these logs. Fasten with either the largest-sized staples or with three-inch nails, bending their top inch down over the wire.

Next, place the heaviest rocks available on the part of the fencing that's nearest the logs, laying two rows horizontally. Make sure they're too large to fall through the wire mesh; if you can get huge ones that will stay put even after the wire has rusted out, that's even better. Pull these rocks out of the nearby water, and never from the bank, which needs all the protection it can get. Removing them from within a few feet of the face of the cribbing helps in another way, too. It reduces the stability of that portion of the stream bottom, helping the current to scour deeper.

The upper layer of logs should be placed exactly on top of the first and fastened in the same manner—except that a second layer of wire is seldom necessary. Top logs should barely break the surface even at low water, so that most flood-borne objects will pass over them. This final position has to be precalculated when digging the trenches for the lower logs.

Once again, place the largest rocks you can handle adjacent to the logs, then slant the rock-fill back so it is higher near the bank. It will pay you to fit the big, marginal rocks as carefully as you would a dry wall, for they too will have to shed high-water flotsam. Finally, plant willow shoots in the rock interstices all over the cribbing and repeat this every spring until you have a dense stand established. In two or three years, these fast-growing plants will catch debris with their trunks and branches and actually increase current deflection in high water. This not only adds to the scouring action, but also helps force destructive objects to swerve away from your cribbing.

Properly positioned, constructed, and planted, a cribbing should last for many years with only minor maintenance and repairs. Several that I have built came through the Act-of-God flood of the summer of '69 with flying colors. Several of my earlier experiments, however, were lost—an experience that gave me some insight into which improvement schemes will stand up and which will not.

If you have the money or the available machinery, you can build all-rock cribbings that will last for generations if installed properly. In shape they should resemble log-faced cribbings; you should position them at the same angle to the current and in similar stretches of the river.

Now for the differences. To build an all-rock cribbing you must first bulldoze the shifting gravel away and get down to sizable rocks; otherwise you'll get so much scour that your structure will topple into its own undermine. And you'll have to use really big rocks. Anything you can budge with a crowbar the stream can move, too. Monoliths the size of a grand piano are perfect and they'll stay put if properly seated.

That's where the expense comes in. Such slabs may have to be trucked to the site, and it takes a good-sized payloader to stack them up. But once they're in you can forget about them. Permanence has its price.

Gabions (fine-mesh wire cages filled with rocks) have very little value as improvers of flood-prone streams. When they deflect enough water to scour a good trench, they tumble into their own handiwork and disappear. They just aren't rigid enough to withstand much undercutting.

Simple deflector and current-directing logs that have proved themselves on more stable waters won't work here, either. They may produce the desired effect at low or medium flow, but under full flood conditions the water roars over them and attacks the bank behind them, increasing the destruction. The down-current ends of all cribbings must therefore be finished off at an obtuse—never an acute—angle to the bank.

There are, however, some less Herculean labors you can perform for a stream that will help it little by little. Willow planting along banks is always good practice since these small trees are water-loving and strong-rooted. Rip-rapping sand banks with large, flat slabs can halt further erosion and siltation downstream.

Large rocks and boulders are always a welcome addition to a stream bed, but the biggest you can roll by human power are barely big enough. (Whatever you do, don't steal them from the nearby banks.) The virtue of large boulders is that they usually produce short, deep scours on their down-current side, while insect-food debris such as dead leaves and twigs catch under their front edges.

If you and your friends (or your club) decide to try to help your favorite streams, there are certain obvious procedures you should follow. Ask permission from your state fish and game commission before you start, since many require permits to tamper with flowing water—even if you're the riparian owner. If your plans are sound, though, they'll usually give you their blessing and add some extremely helpful advice.

If you lease the water or merely have permission to fish it, by all means get the owner's approval as well. Again, if your projects offer real improvement, he can hardly raise any valid objection.

When you've been given the go-ahead, resist the temptation to rush into construction. First, draw up a master plan for the area you're going to improve. Observe and take notes on this water at least once when it's in flood or running extremely high. This will not only impress you with the forces that your future structures will have to contend with, but it may also give you a new understanding of how the river cuts when it's actually working. And there's much to be learned from studying productive pools and runs in low water, when you can analyze the high-water forces that dug them and keep them scoured clean.

Finally, start your first project at a tight-banked, relatively stable location. It's heartbreaking to slave over a cribbing only to discover, the following season, that the river has cut itself a new channel, leaving your good works high and dry on the gravel. For the same reason, work in a progressive downstream direction. Your first cribbing may deflect the current to the opposite bank, and it's vital to know this before starting your next structure.

I have built several cribbings single-handedly (despite what my children and weekend guests may tell you), but extra hands do make the work quicker and pleasanter. Machinery, as I've said, can do wonders if you're willing to pay the price. A backhoe can dig deep trenches in a short time, and a payloader can pile on all the ballast you'll need (*after* you've hand-fitted the big, outside rocks) in a few hours. With this sort of help—and expense—it's possible to complete a cribbing in a day if you have prearranged all the materials and planned the construction properly.

What sort of reward, in terms of actual fish, can you expect from the finished product? It all depends on the stream you're working with and on the existing number of fish in the river available for attraction. Even a simple cribbing can hold several good (more than twelve-inch) fish despite the territorial aggressiveness of trout. On a rare, perfect evening, I have caught five in a row without moving my feet from one such structure and I'm not sure I didn't put down more before I could cover them. A compound cribbing, as I've mentioned before, may hold twice as many.

A compound cribbing created my all-time favorite fishing place. Upstream from where I like to stand, the water breaks over a diagonal riffle that bunches the thread of the current sharply toward the bank to my right. While the water is still dancing and deepening, it meets the first log which angles out slightly from the bank. The flow hugs this log for twenty feet or more, slows down into a smooth glide, and hits the second log, which juts out more sharply. The current gradually quickens again until it boils out past the end of this last log and shallows out into another riffle. For nearly 50 feet, the water near the logs is three to three-and-a-half feet deep; it fishes like a short pool in low water, like a deep run when the river's up.

This place has everything a trout could ask for. There's a food-producing riffle directly above, a concentrated feed lane of drift food, and cover enough under the logs and between the rocks to hide even some full-grown salmon. It's ideal for the fisherman, too. Your presentations here are almost drag-free, for the current moves past you like a turning wheel—slowest at the hub where you stand and fastest out on the rim where your fly is being cast.

Cribbings have one other big advantage: they can stretch the length of your good-fishing season. Brown trout have two main migration periods. First, they move upstream for cooler water and safer depths during the first hint of drought in early summer. A good undercut can hold some of these fish all summer, keeping them from pushing on through to spring-holes and feeder creeks. Their second big migration is in the fall, during September and October, when all the mature fish in the stream seem to play musical chairs. Your fishing season may now be over, but cribbings provide ideal wintering spots and will hold large fish upriver for your early spring fishing—trout that might otherwise head down to the big water after spawning.

Is this sort of work worth all the backaches and blisters? It all depends on your available time, temperament, and long-range commitment to trout fishing. The facts show that the number of fishermen is increasing every year by leaps and bounds while the amount of available trout water is probably shrinking. Don't let the antipollution bills—good as they are—mislead you. Even if they're carried out to the letter, they will do far more to reclaim larger rivers for warm-water species than they will to expand upland trout waters. In the meantime, we'll probably keep losing water to the dammers and developers.

Probably every generation has complained about the fishing, wishing for the good old days. An Elizabethan poet, 375 years ago, wrote:

> *Fishing, if I, a fisher, may protest,*
> *Of pleasures is the sweetest, of*
> *sports the best. . . .*
> *But now the sport is marde, and*
> *wott ye why?*
> *Fishes decrease, and fishers*
> *multiply.*

He had no idea how good he had it. But lamenting and viewing with alarm are no answer. Obviously, as a trout fisherman, you should support all good conservation measures and ecology-minded candidates. Certainly you should join Trout Unlimited, the Federation of Fly Fishers, and any organization dedicated to the future of your sport.

But perhaps you should get even more deeply involved with some local grass-roots—or rather, willow-roots—work on your favorite stream. This is the only way to produce more trout per existing mile of running water. And, if you shuttle the current back and forth from bank to bank artfully enough, you just might create a few more miles of trout fishing, too.

1977

PART 2

8

The Deadliest Lure

If you think that fly fishers avoid lures
and live bait for ethical or conservation
reasons—think again.

There is a popular notion that fly fishermen are people who nobly impose an artificial handicap on themselves to make the catching of fish more difficult. But it just isn't so. Fly fishing may be noble in its ideals; it is also devastatingly effective. In an appropriate form and properly fished, flies offer sport that cannot be duplicated by the wood, metal, or plastic gadgetry of other lures. Consider the evidence. For trout, the case is easy to build. Flies were originated to kill trout. The fragile aquatic insects which are the staple trout diet break up when skewered on a hook. Something more durable had to be created—and created it was, some two thousand years ago according to surviving records, and perhaps artificial flies were no novelty even then. The worm and the minnow may have their innings under certain conditions, but the fly is the most consistent trout killer and has been for centuries.

No less an authority than Edward R. Hewitt stated that the skillful nymph fisherman was the only man who could clean a stream of sophisticated brown trout by legal angling. And the nymph, though a fairly recent refinement, is very much a fly and in the classic tradition of close imitation.

Further proof is provided by the fact that professional fishermen use flies, perhaps not exclusively but very regularly. In France, anglers who make a living by supplying restaurants with wild trout taken from heavily fished public streams use flies most of the time. In high water or when they're after a specific large fish, they may turn to the spun minnow, but they earn their daily French bread during most of the season with the fly. And I might add that the best of them may be the finest trout fishermen in the world.

The same is true in Spain. Men who fish the few public salmon rivers in the north use flies regularly when the water is neither too roily nor too deep. And when you consider that the average Spanish salmon can be sold for as much as a laborer earns in two months of hard work, you can be sure that the fly is no affectation there.

Trout and salmon may be the traditional victims of the fly, but all gamefish, except perhaps those that live in unreachable depths are highly susceptible to fur and feathers. Spinners, plugs, and naturals are not so universally effective, regardless of what their adherents may claim. New York State employs an expert fisherman to check populations of lakes, ponds, and streams and to catch fish for scale samples. His quarry are mainly smallmouth and largemouth bass, yet he uses a fly rod exclusively and claims that an orange streamer is his most effective lure.

Even commercial tuna fishermen in the Pacific use flies. For on the end of those two- and three-pole rigs with which they yank tuna into the boat there is a special quick-release hook covered with white feathers. And large white-feathered jigs have been used for decades by sport fishermen and commercial trollers.

Of course, the flies just described wouldn't be recognized as such under a New England covered bridge. Are, then, these large minnow and squid imitations really flies? In one sense yes, and in another no. The Spanish say no. They make a clear distinction that is surprising for a country not noted for its sport fishing. There, a fly that imitates an insect is properly called a *mosca*, while a streamer or salmon fly is a *pluma*. I think they are right in calling one the fly and the other the feather, but our own language has no such nicety.

However, the English definition has its merits, too. Both the dainty insect imitation and the large feather squid owe their effectiveness to the same qualities—qualities that separate them from live bait, spinners, or solid wobbling plugs. First and foremost of these is the action of feather, fur, and hair. They breathe, wiggle, and kick in a unique manner when drawn through the water. And perhaps equally important, all these materials are translucent in the water, as are the insects, minnows, elvers, or squid that they counterfeit.

In the beginning, of course, was the wet trout fly. In fact, until about a hundred years ago it was *the* fly. The great blossoming into many styles for many types of fishing is a rather recent development, and testifies to the high quality of the materials that flies are made of.

The artificial nymph, for instance, is merely a refinement of the basic wet fly, and it came out of England at the turn of the century. Probably the great Frederick Halford of dry-fly fame was indirectly responsible for its development, although he was to fight till his dying day against the use of nymphs. It was Halford who established the doctrine of exact mimicry in dry-fly fishing. So successful was he in implanting this ideal that wet-fly fishermen took to more exact imitation of the underwater, or nymphal, forms of aquatic insects. Under the leadership of G. E. M. Skues, the nymph fishermen fought the Halfordians for over a quarter of a century. While neither side ever won a clear-cut victory, the literature that resulted is some of the most spirited in the entire angling library. Since the turn of the century, the nymph has appeared in a wide variety of patterns. It is not only a recent invention but an extremely important one, for Hewitt was right in his estimate of its efficiency on wary fish such as the brown trout.

The streamer fly and its cousin the bucktail are purely American in origin. One story has it that a man was fishing with a large wet fly when the throat hackle broke, unwound, and streamed out behind the fly. This accidental lure was an immediate success and an idea was born. After all, big trout and landlocked salmon feed heavily on minnows, and a hackle feather of suitable color, undulating along the hook shank, makes a very likely imitation, as we now know. However, the story is considered apocryphal. Officially, the streamer is credited to Maine fly tyer Herb Welsh, and the date is recorded as 1901.

The bass fly was also developed in this country. In its older, purer forms, it is basically a huge trout-type wet fly, usually in one of the brighter patterns and dressed as fully as possible to make it a chunky mouthful. You don't see this type of fly around much anymore, though. The big streamer fly has largely replaced it. And the exciting surface lures of clipped deer hair are becoming more popular each season. They mimic such delicacies of the bass menu as frogs, dragonflies, crayfish, and even mice. If hair-and-feather minnows and squid are to be considered flies, then these hair-bodied counterfeits would also seem to fit the category. And they do catch fish with gratifying regularity.

But unquestionably the most important fly development in recorded history is the dry fly. Here, too, there has been progress in recent years but, surprisingly, not because of any great advances in the science of entomology. Ronalds' *The Fly-fisher's Entomology* was published in England in 1836 and is still widely quoted. While it may be a taxonomist's horror (it avoids Latin names, preferring terms like Pale Watery Dun), it speaks the angler's language. In America we have no such single standard work. There have been valiant attempts like Ernest Schwiebert's *Matching the Hatch* and Art Flick's *Streamside Guide to Naturals and Their Imitations*. Schwiebert dealt with the entire United States, while Flick limited himself to New York's Catskills. Both books are often very useful. Yet I know a stream ecologically similar to Flick's Scoharie, and not forty miles from it, where half of the important insects bear no resemblance to Flick's favored dozen. Apparently, America is too huge, too rich, and too diverse a habitat for any one man to entomologize. This may be an argument in favor of the slight leaning toward impressionism discernible in many modern American flies.

There has also been a trend toward drabness, simply because drab flies seem to work well on our streams. No longer are flies designed primarily for brook trout in ponds, as they once were, because the ecological picture has changed. The colorful artificials which were used for that purpose evolved into bass flies.

Finally, there has been a trend toward chunky, less delicate dry flies on both sides of the Atlantic, and this has a simple explanation. Trout streams in most well-populated countries have a higher percentage of newly stocked fish each year. These trout must remember the hatchery mouthful better than the mayfly. They simply go for something that looks like an insect and is fat enough to rivet their attention. The highly selective wild brown trout of Halford's day are now hard to find, and today's flies reflect this change in conditions.

Furthermore, many more fish are considered game species now than in the late nineteenth century, and many more sportsmen have learned to use the fly rod. This has resulted in an incredible proliferation of both classic patterns and relatively new ones. Even if a fisherman finds himself on strange water with nothing to match the hatch precisely, he can switch from fly to fly until he finds a good one, or he can shop for local patterns. Being inexpensive, flies encourage experimentation.

Of course, certain of the oldest classic patterns are still with us in pretty much their original form—dry flies like the famous Blue Dun, wets like the Wickham's Fancy, Coachman, Leadwing Coachman, and Royal Coachman. They are far too effective to be forsaken. But excellence has not hindered experimentation. For instance, it was discovered quite early that some dry flies could be tied as wet patterns to imitate drowned insects. Hence, we have both wet and dry versions of the great Quill Gordon, Light Cahill, Greenwell's Glory, Gold-Ribbed Hare's Ear, plus many newer patterns.

Through experimentation by anglers and professional fly tyers, the list is constantly lengthened. Among the relatively new and vastly popular wets are Fledermaus, the Muddler Minnow streamers, and the woven hair-bodied nymphs that are now being used extensively in the Rockies. And recent years have brought fame to such dry patterns as the Rat-Faced Macdougal, Gray Wulff (and other Wulff variations), Jassid, Irresistible, and a whole batch of small midges and terrestrial insects, such as beetles and ants. These little terrestrials, which originated with the "Pennsylvania school" of fly tyers, have provided still further possibilities for dry-fly experimentation.

The name of the actual inventor of dry flies has been lost—if, indeed, one person was the inventor. Late in the nineteenth century a number of factors made the development of the dry fly almost inevitable. One was the introduction of the split-cane fly rod. Here was an instrument that could not only reach out to shy fish in clear, low water, but could also flick the droplets off a fly and dry it on the false cast. Then came the vacuum-dressed silk line that brought out the potential of the bamboo as the older braided horsehair and linen lines never could. And perhaps most important of all was Henry Sinclair Hall's perfection of the mass-produced, eyed trout hook. Before it appeared on the market in 1879, trout hooks were "blind." Their tapered shanks were whipped to a piece of gut or to a single strand of horsehair. Changing a sodden fly for a fresh one under those circumstances meant changing the leader, or at least part of it. Without the eyed hook, dry-fly fishing would have been too tedious to become popular. And it was with the rising popularity of the dry fly late in the last half of the nineteenth century that the hackle feather became the rightful center of fly-tying attention. For a dry fly must float on its hackle tips, and most of its effectiveness depends on hackle quality and color.

Halford and his crew of dry-fly zealots had little difficulty obtaining their feathers. Since their numbers were small, their demands were not large. As a matter of doctrine, they cast only to rising fish; this meant that even mediocre hackle could be used, because the fly had long periods of inactivity in which to dry off. Lastly, cock fighting had been abolished as recently as 1849, and many a stiff-hackled cock still strutted the British barnyards.

The dry fly was launched in America in 1885, when Halford sent a set of his dry flies to Theodore Gordon in New York State. Gordon was an inventive and observant sportsman. He realized that Halford's flies imitated British insects and that insects on this side of the Atlantic were quite different. He originated many impressionistic imitations of the naturals he found on his own favorite streams—the Quill Gordon being perhaps the most famous of his patterns. His flies seem a bit large-winged to us today, and the style of winging has changed slightly, but the present-day master tyers of the Catskills carry on his basic tradition.

The first American book on dry-fly fishing didn't appear until some twenty years after Gordon began his experiments, and by the time the dry fly became really popular here, a bit after World War I, the materials situation was becoming acute. First, American demands on hackle were far more severe than Britain's. Our streams are more turbulent than Halford's stately chalkstreams. Only the very stiffest hackle would do. Then, too, our insects are larger, and a bigger, heavier hook has to be supported. And, finally, casting only to the rise doesn't work well here. An angler must prospect likely water in our mountain streams, rise or no rise. So the fly must float, cast after cast, with only a false cast or two to dry it.

Even today, there is no synthetic dry-fly hackle on the market, nor any miracle chemical that can transform soft hackle into needle-sharp barbs. Superb hackle can float a fly unaided, but the pioneer dry-fly anglers in England often resorted to coating the hackle with paraffin solutions. Theodore Gordon frequently used kerosene. Until a few years ago, standard fly-line dressing was dissolved in gasoline or the less flammable carbon tet. Now we have the superior silicone preparations, which represent another advance in fly fishing, but this is not to say the problem has been solved. Poor hackle still floats poorly.

By the time the dry fly gained wide acceptance in America, the source of hackle supply was diminishing. Not only had cock fighting long been outlawed here, but the agricultural revolution had transformed chicken-raising into a mass-production industry, to the detriment of the hackle supply. Birds were now bred for fast growth and plump breasts, or for greater egg production. Certainly not for first-class hackles. And to top it all off, most cockerels were killed for fryers when only months old.

To see the full implications of this fly tyer's nightmare, you must understand a few facts about the nature of the bird that bears the indispensable hackle. All of our current breeds of chickens are descendants of a wild bird from India called the Bankiva fowl. The males of the species are extremely polygamous and, hence, highly combative. While the females have unimposing neck feathers, the males have long, stiff, glossy hackles, which protect the vulnerable neck and throat area from the leg spurs and beaks of rivals. Since the bird that survives the fight gets the hens and begets the chicks, birds with the stiffest neck feathers prospered. The process of natural selection toward stiff neck feathers was started in the wild and continued until cock fighting was outlawed. Then the purveyors of eggs and white meat stepped in, and the tyer had to scout the ever-decreasing subsistence farms for a source of supply.

How then, you may ask, is the current army of several million fly fishermen supplied? The answer is, poorly—except for the anglers who deal with top custom tyers. General stores, hardware stores, and even sports shops have to take what they can get.

Most of the hackle is soft, and half of it has been dyed—a process that further reduces the quality of already indifferent hackle. The necks are bought in bulk from importers who buy them by the hundreds of thousands in India. Most of these necks are ginger, red, or white—useful colors, but not the full spectrum a tyer would like. A few of the necks are first-rate, and you're fortunate if you can pick and choose from a boxful. But commercial houses can't afford such sorting and discarding. Surprisingly, top-notch flies can still be obtained if you know the right professional tyer. There are a few of these men left, yet very few young tyers are coming up. The reason is that there's no money in producing quality flies.

A tyer must raise most of his own roosters. True, some necks in the more common colors can be picked up from a friendly

importer, but none is likely to be found in the all-important shades
called natural duns. These are a slaty blue-gray color, and fly tyers
have made their reputations on their dun hackles. To get such hackles, birds must be bred, crossbred, pampered, and plucked, and the
price of doing this is almost confiscatory. Yet nearly half of the most
popular dry flies call for this shade, and a dyed feather always shows
a bogus blue or purplish tinge when held up to the light—which is
precisely how a trout sees it.

To get the natural duns, you have to raise a lot of birds. About
fifty percent of the eggs hatched will produce cocks, but only a few
of them will have top-quality hackle. Then, too, the blue-dun color
is recessive. No matter how you breed, you'll end up with lots of
badger (white with black center), black, and white hackles. Only a
small percentage will be true duns.

I once asked an acknowledged master, Harry Darbee of Liv-
ingston Manor, New York, how he bred his magnificent dun roosters. He was a bit guarded about just how he has built up a superior
strain after some thirty years of continuous breeding, but he did
tell me that he has to breed back in a Cochin strain from time to
time to keep the feathers in the small, usable sizes and to keep up
the steely quality. But what is his ratio of duns to the less useful
colors? His answer was, "Man, do we eat a lot of chicken!"

Since I myself have raised birds for hackles, I can readily understand the economic plight of the professional tyer. It cost me $10
a year per rooster just for the special small-grain feed that hackle-
producing birds are supposed to have. It takes two years for birds
to reach full maturity, so a bird has eaten $20 worth of feed before
he starts producing.

With luck, a bird should produce excellent hackle for several
years. A prize rooster is seldom killed; he is plucked with tender,
loving care three or four times a year.

Curiously, despite the costs and risks of trying to raise excellent hackle, flies tied with these superior materials by the finest
artists of the day cost only pennies more than run-of-the-mill shop-
tied flies. I once asked Walt Dette, the master fly tyer of Roscoe,

New York, why this should be so. "It's all the traffic will bear," he explained. "After all, trout flies are expendable. The average guy leaves several of them in trees during a day's fishing. Who'd pay a buck for a fly?"

There is only one factor that sweetens the pot for independent, custom tyers like Darbee and Dette. There's no middleman. The feathers go straight from rooster to fisherman, and fly tyer takes all. Even so, most fly tyers drive old cars. And the finest craftsman that I ever knew gave it all up to work in a barbershop a few years back. Once a man has paid for the hooks, thread, wax, and other purchasable materials—not to mention the costs of rooster-raising—he can't tie much more than $5 or $6 worth (circa 1970) of flies in an hour. If machines were available, the economic picture might be brighter. But every fly must be tied from start to finish by hand.

What, then, keeps the few remaining perfectionists in the business? Pride, certainly. The good life, probably, too. Tyers live near good fishing and shooting. But there seems to be more to it than that. They are celebrities in the eyes of dedicated fishermen. Their advice is sought by presidents and board chairmen. You stand in line to get their flies and you don't dare annoy them even if your order doesn't arrive by opening day.

Since the basic materials of most flies have always come from the barnyard, it's natural that there's a touch of barnyard earthiness in some of the flies themselves. One all-time favorite is named the Cow Dung because it imitates a green-bodied fly that is usually found on meadow muffins. Another classic is the Tup's Indispensable, invented by R. S. Austin of Tiverton in Devon. The exact dressing of this killing fly was a closely kept secret for years. Sound business was one reason. Victorian prudery another. For how would you explain to a nineteenth-century gentlewoman that the beautifully translucent yellow body was dubbed with urine-stained hair taken from the indispensable portion of a ram, or tup?

The famous Hendrickson dry fly originated by Roy Steenrod, an early pupil of Theodore Gordon's, has a similar origin. The body is dubbed with fur from the crotch of a red fox vixen, which has a permanent pink stain.

Those are some of the more esoteric materials—including a few of the most expensive ones. Feathers, and particularly hackles, are still pivotal to fly tying and to fly fishing, but long evenings at the tying vice produce a lot of experimentation. In streamer flies, maribou stork feathers with their octopuslike action are rivaling bucktail and saddle hackles. Silk floss and similar body materials have always had their place, but newer materials are now finding other uses. For instance, tarnish-proof strips of Mylar tinsel are showing up more and more in the wings of these flies.

Bucktail flies obviously get their name from the deer tail of which they're made, and this material has always been plentiful. Because of its texture, consistency, and length, it is valuable for many wet-fly effects. In a way, its versatility makes it more valuable than that special hair from a vixen. The deer hair that's being displaced nowadays in streamers is popping up in, of all places, dry-fly dressing. Many of the shaggy but effective Wulff flies have bucktail tails and wings. Harry Darbee's inspired Rat-Faced Macdougal and the series of variations that have followed it sport bodies of clipped deer hair.

These flies may be a bit chunky for delicate mayfly imitations, but they are the only flies that will float in a downpour. And since a pelting rain can knock enough insects out of the bushes to make a pool boil, such flies represent another deadly set of lures.

In wet flies, fluorescent flosses are also appearing these days—particularly in the bodies of salmon flies. They give off a glow on dark days or in the depths, causing many anglers to swear by them. Synthetics aren't really new; J. W. Dunne of England popularized them back in the twenties. In *Sunshine and the Dry-Fly*, he advocated a series of artificials with bodies of cellulite floss over white-painted hook shanks. When anointed with oil, these bodies had a succulent translucency. They haven't been on the market since World War II, but new types of brightly glowing synthetics are being tied into wet patterns.

These changes in materials and in flies tell a lot about trends in fishing. Most of Halford's original split-wing floaters were winged with dun-colored starling primary feathers and epitomized the ultrarealistic approach. Theodore Gordon leaned toward bunched wood-duck flank feathers glimpsed through the hackle. He was an impressionist. Darbee's Rat-Face and the Wulff flies are highly utilitarian and offer a good mouthful. Experimenting with shapes can probably go just so far, but experimenting with materials, from the dullest to the most garishly fluorescent will probably never end.

Happily, the materials used for wet flies, nymphs, and streamers, whether new or old in dressing style, remain in good supply. A Royal Coachman, for instance, utilizes golden-pheasant tippet, peacock herl, red silk floss, red-brown cock or hen hackle, and white primary goose or duck quill. A fly tyer has little trouble obtaining these items.

Salmon-fly materials felt the pinch early in this century when many feathers were proscribed by international treaties. Indian crow, cock of the rock, toucan, and bustard disappeared from the salmon-fly repertory, but suitable and effective substitutes have been found and the fully dressed fly of today is hard to distinguish from its nineteenth-century prototype (though smaller, less fully dressed salmon flies have also gained wide acceptance).

Fortunately, the banned feathers were used mainly as color accents. The most widely used exotics—golden pheasant, jungle cock, English jay, summer duck, florican, European kingfisher, blue-and-yellow and red-and-yellow macaw, silver pheasant, and the rest—are still available to fly tyers even though they can be quite expensive.

The demand for these materials is not increasing, because salmon-fishing tactics have changed considerably. In the good old days, it was mainly an early spring and late fall sport. Salmon were considered uncatchable in low water and warm weather. The British now use smaller, less colorful, more sparsely dressed flies during the summer and have opened up a whole new season for the sport. And in Canada the fishing is mostly from late June through September, and the same small, relatively drab flies are now most popular there, too.

Most of these flies are winged with hair or with the natural plumage of various ducks like widgeon, teal, and mallard. Usually such feathers are relatively easy to obtain from hunting friends, but bulk shipments from overseas are under continuous attack by the National Audubon Society. While the Society's main objection is to the use of the feathers by the millinery trade, tyers feel threatened, too.

The Audubon people are worthy opponents. A few years ago an Audubon friend of mine told me with some satisfaction that a member of his chapter was head inspector of feathers for the New York customs department. "You fly tyers can't fool him," he claimed. "Why, he can tell what kind of bird almost any feather comes from, and you can bet he catches lots of contraband shipments." I had the last word, though. I told him that a fifth-generation salmon-fly tyer I knew who came from Ireland could do that dead drunk. And, when sober, this man could tell which square inch of the bird the feather came from and estimate the bird's age accurately! He really could, too.

Of course, these economic and legal tugs of war that plague the fly tyer are little noticed by the world at large. Only once, to my knowledge, did fly tying hit the headlines. Late in the last century, a man was killed in northern Ireland following a heated discussion about the precise shade of dyed seal's fur that should be used in dubbing the body of Michael Rogan's Fiery Brown salmon fly. However, one has to suspect that some fiery brown liquid may have been more to blame for this crime of passion than the fly itself.

When fly tyers and fly fishermen do make news, it is generally conservation news which appears in publications devoted to the subject or is, unfortunately, relegated to the back pages of the papers. For these men are extremely active in conservation groups that fight pollution, wanton industrial development of wild areas, and similar threats to wildlife. And even though flies are so deadly in expert hands that they may, as Hewitt stated, take every trout in a stream, the fly fisherman is the trout's best friend. He may catch 90 percent of the trout that are netted on our hard-fished streams, but he understands that running water will support only so many fish, and he knows of the scarcity of running water itself. He releases most of the fish he catches, to avoid depleting a limited population.

His sport allows him to do so, and this is another angling advance that is virtually unique to the fly. A fly-caught fish is almost always lip-hooked and easy to release. Treble-hook plugs and spoons and bait hooks which are easily swallowed are another matter. Studies have shown that nearly half of all worm-hooked, undersized trout soon die. The comparative figure for fly-hooked fish is three percent, and this estimate is not restricted just to barbless flies; the figure would be much lower for the many fly fishermen who carefully remove the barbs from their hooks.

So, even though the lure may be deadly, the man may be merciful. And there's wisdom in this. It's better to enjoy golden eggs than to eat goose.

1970

9

Angling's
Forgotten Fly

Surprisingly, only twenty-five years ago,
you couldn't find a floating caddis imitation,
much less tips on how to fish it.

Fly fishermen are like everyone else in that they thrive on success and wilt under defeat. In fact, if it weren't for the occasional
red-letter day, I doubt that many of us would keep so doggedly at
it, year after year. Yet our successes probably do more to warm our
hearts than to stir our minds. For it usually takes total, dismal
defeat to start us thinking and experimenting. At least, this is true
in my case. The most rewarding type of trout fishing I now enjoy
can be traced back directly to a black, blank day more than twenty
years ago.

I had been pounding away with little hope on the lower Beaverkill
on a raw and blustery day when a dramatic change occurred. Just
as the sun went down the wind dropped with it and there was a sudden softness to the air. For one of the few times in my life I felt,
with that unnamed sense most animals seem to have, that something

important in nature was about to happen. Soon swallows began working the river excitedly and in a few minutes flies began to appear, first in twos and threes, then by dozens and hundreds. To this day I have never seen such a hatch of flies! They swarmed past me upstream, the highest thirty feet or so above my head, the lowest ricocheting along the river's surface. The flat water around me churned with feeding trout, some leaping, some slashing, some just lipping the surface. I tied on a dun that seemed about right for size and color and went to work on a large fish I'd marked down. He picked up naturals so close to my fly that he rocked it several times. Once he even bunted it with his nose. But he never made the fatal mistake. I switched to other smaller trout nearby with the same result. Finally, as darkness fell, I was casting with random desperation—hoping for one foolish fish of any size. I must have covered a hundred rising trout in that hour without a single take! I finally left the river in pitch darkness, arm-weary and too defeated even to find comfort in cursing.

One thing that I had done was right, though. During a spell of utter despair I had stopped casting long enough to trap a few specimens in my hat and stuff them into a fly box. Later that night I examined the captives as they crawled through a compartment filled with Quill Gordons. The color wasn't a bad match, and the size #14 I'd been using seemed about right. But beyond that, everything was hopelessly wrong. In the first place, the wings of the naturals seemed opaque, not translucent. More important, they were furled horizontally, almost enveloping the body. And these insects had long feelers in front, but no tails. All the flies in my boxes had longish tails and Marconi-rigged wings for, like almost all dry flies dressed today, they were designed to imitate some mayfly or other. And mayflies look nothing at all like the flies I'd just captured, for the latter belonged to a very different order of insects called the Trichoptera, or caddisflies.

Surprisingly, not one of the fifty or one hundred most popular dry flies of the day is tied in the distinctive caddis shape. And yet, the caddis runs the mayfly a very close second as the trout's most important food insect. In some acid water it may well be the more important of the two. Louis Rhead, writing near the turn of the century, devoted a large section of his book to one species of caddis alone. "The Shad-fly is the most abundant trout insect food that appears in our Eastern and some Middle and Far Western streams. Trout are ravenous for it," he writes; but he adds, "When the great rise appears it is hardly possible to catch a trout with any prevailing artificial as now tied." Some three-quarters of a century later, this brownish caddis is still extremely abundant in New York's Delaware watershed, where Rhead so often fished. And it is still one of the most baffling hatches to fly fishermen, mainly because it is not a mayfly but a caddis.

Yet, anglers have not always ignored, or been ignorant of, the caddis. Not long before Rhead's time, the caddis played a pivotal role in American fly fishing. It seems that, for all our progress, we have forgotten some things that our great-grandfathers considered elementary. So, if we backtrack a century or so, perhaps we may find a way to restore this valuable insect to our repertory.

By the time trout fishing emerged as a sport in America, the fish-gathering of colonial times had already taken its toll. Contrary to the popular impression, mid-nineteenth century sportsmen did not live in a fisherman's paradise. Already, most major rivers had been dammed or polluted beyond the tolerance of salmon or trout. While small streams near home may have still run clear, cool, and uncluttered by tin cans, they now held only tiddling brook trout best left to small boys and village idlers. But there remained a vast semiwilderness not too far away. Real fishing meant a trip to Maine, to the Adirondacks, or to Canada. Here were chains of clear lakes or peaty ponds relatively unfished by today's standards and teeming with wild brook trout, some of which were very large. Weekend buggy excursions were out. This sort of fishing meant long trips with guides and long stays under canvas. Winslow Homer caught the tail end of this era and his watercolors can tell you as much about it as any book. Sportsmen fished these still waters the way their ancestors had fished the lakes and lochs of Great Britain—

with a technique, by the way, that is used in Scotland to this day. And the transplanted method worked. For these relatively infertile, acid waters on both sides of the Atlantic had this in common: Caddis were major food factors in both.

By sheer chance, I once happened to witness this earlier style of fishing, though at the time I didn't realize the significance of what I was seeing. Years ago, some family friends invited me for a two-week stay on a remote lake in a large Adirondack preserve. They said the lake was teeming with trout, but admitted they didn't fish very much themselves. I arrived in late July with a short, stiff dry-fly rod, double-tapered silk line, tapered gut leaders, brand new Hardy dry flies, and enough self-confidence for the whole party. The feeling that I'd be taking advantage of these unsophisticated brook trout increased when I saw the tackle my hosts used. Their rods were nine to ten feet long and as limp as grapevines. Windings were frayed and varnish was chipped or nonexistent. Some were made of solid wood and didn't even have cork grips. And that was just the beginning. Reels were toy-sized and held only a few yards of thin, cracked enamel line. On the end of these rigs were the heaviest level leaders I'd ever seen, each sporting a team of three large, snelled wet flies. Everything looked as though it had been borrowed from the Smithsonian. My host admitted that these outfits had been kicking around for years and years but added that they still worked surprisingly well.

After supper that first evening, six of us piled into three canoes and paddled uplake to a wide, alder-lined inlet flowage. I immediately began casting my perky little dry fly to likely looking spots, but, to my astonishment, I didn't see or get a rise. The others didn't even pick up their rods until just at dusk when flies and rising trout appeared as suddenly as if some hidden signal had been given. I soon noticed, to my chagrin, that everyone else was hauling in fish. My frequently cast dry fly just sat there rocking on the ripples set up by the trout rising all around it. The others were making ridiculously short casts and trickling the flies back over the surface not more than a dozen feet from their canoes. And they were hooking fish almost every time they cast.

If I remember correctly, everyone else caught a dozen or more fat, dark trout running from half a pound to slightly more than a pound, while I managed to land one six-incher just at dark. Needless to say, I borrowed one of those archaic rigs and learned how to dance the dropper properly, making it zigzag over the surface like the caddisflies that miraculously appeared at the same hour each evening. But the experience made little or no impression on me at the same time. The fishing was so different from anything I'd ever seen before that I crossed it off as one of those baffling exceptions that prove the rule. Looking back now, though, that nineteenth-century tackle made a lot of sense for that specialized type of fishing. The rod was long to keep the flies as far as possible from the boat. It was limber to impart a jiggling motion to the dropper and to prevent a smash when a large fish walloped the fly. The line was light and level to keep it from bellying down close to the boat. And the flies were on heavy snells so that they would stand out away from the leader and dance properly. The heaviness of the leader itself didn't seem to put the fish off because the bottom two flies were rarely taken. Their main function was to set up enough drag in the water to tighten line and leader during the retrieve. When the rod was held high and the tip wobbled by the angler, it was the skittering top dropper that captured the trout's attention. When you see the stunt performed properly you realize that the hand of man can't better this impression of a caddis buzzing over the surface.

Despite my chance encounter with it, this kind of fly fishing had begun to disappear rapidly some eighty years ago, and you'd have to look far and wide to find it anywhere today. For three events occurred in rapid succession that changed American fly fishing, perhaps forever.

First came the transplanting of the smallmouth black bass from the Mississippi watershed into the lakes of the Northeast. Bass are great gamefish in their own right, but they're too much competition for the slower-growing brook trout. Squaretail populations dropped off rapidly in the newly stocked waters, and the lakes that still held trout just couldn't absorb the increased pressure. Despite vigorous restocking, stillwater trout fishing in New York and New England has-n't recovered to this day. Second, the hardy, fast-growing brown trout from Europe was introduced into our less-polluted streams and rivers at about the same time. Why travel all the way to the now-uncertain waters of northern Maine when you could catch three-pound trout after a two- or three-hour train ride? Advanced fly fishers turned to the challenge of brown trout and began to focus on running-water techniques. Third, well-informed anglers quickly borrowed sophisticated European techniques to deal with the imported trout. In came the new orthodoxy fresh from the pages of Halford and the chalk-streams of England. Long, limber rods and light lines began to gather dust in attics. The new rod must be stiff, the line heavy, the leader tapered to the finest point. The single fly must float, and float absolutely dead-drift.

It worked, of course. Yet something had been lost. True, men like Gordon, La Branche, and Hewitt modified chalkstream dogma to suit American conditions and they made magnificent contributions. But perhaps they didn't go far enough, because they all forgot the caddisfly.

Probably the most logical explanation for this enormous omission is that these great fishermen all started with the Halford doctrine and changed it only when necessity dictated. It is interesting to speculate on what American dry-fly fishing might have been like today if it had sprung up spontaneously under our conditions and on our rivers. For consider the gap that must be bridged between, say, the Beaverkill in New York and the Test in Hampshire, England. The Test is one of the richest rivers in the world, chemically. It never suffers from scouring floods and is literally paved with weeds. It teems with mayfly life. As a result, the average two-year-old Test trout will weigh a full two pounds. The Beaverkill, on the other hand, is acid, lacking in the rich carbonates of chalkstreams. It is subjected to several destructive floods each year and has almost no weeds at all. Here a two-year-old trout will weigh only a very few ounces. Obviously, the ecology and entomology of this spartan environment is quite different. Mayfly life is much less profuse, while the acid-tolerant caddis takes on added importance.

Admittedly, the Test had a good caddis population, too. But with endless squadrons of mayfly duns floating down to the waiting trout, Halford gave caddis a very minor place. They were rowdy intruders into his serenely ordered scheme of things. He grudgingly included five caddis patterns in his final selection of forty-three dry flies as some sort of last-ditch remedy when darkness and total defeat were fast enveloping the angler. Mayfly imitations and the fishing of them absolutely dead-drift occupied Halford's missionary zeal for the last twenty years of his influential life.

But at least Halford carried five caddis dry-fly patterns. Can the American trouter, who casts his flies on waters where caddis abound, afford to ignore this type of fly completely? And why, with so many caddis buzzing around him, does he continue to do so? The most obvious reason is, I think, that many anglers simply fail to recognize caddis when they see them. They may be familiar with the log-cabin cases of the larvae and quite able to pick out the winged adults in an illustration. But many otherwise expert anglers are weak on "aircraft identification." And it is surprising how few bother to capture specimens for a closer look. Yet the three basic types of aquatic insects that interest fishermen most are easily identifiable on the wing, even at a considerable distance. In fact, the mayflies, caddisflies, and stoneflies have quite different appearances and characteristics all through their life cycles, and perhaps it's time for a brief review of these differences.

Stoneflies have the least complicated life history. The eggs hatch into larvae, or creepers, and continue growth in this vigorous and mobile form until they are ready for the winged adult stage. Many species then crawl out of the water and emerge from the creeper skin while on shore, but some seem to swim up and undergo this transformation at the water's surface. The adult has two short tails and carries its wings folded flat along its hack when at rest. It is easy to distinguish in the air because it flies rather awkwardly with its body in a vertical position, and all four wings are visible separately as they flail the air.

The mayfly spends its underwater life as a nymph that may take a wide variety of shapes but is always distinguishable from the stonefly creepers because nymphs have their gills on their abdomens while stonefly gills are on the thorax. Most mayflies hatch into duns, or subimagoes, at the water's surface, although a few crawl ashore for this metamorphosis. From this point on, mayflies are easy to identify because they carry their wings erect, like sails over their backs when at rest, and have two or three long thin tails. Mayfly duns are weak fliers and can be readily identified by the fact that they appear to have two translucent wings and hold their bodies nearly horizontal in flight. After a day or so they undergo a second transformation, shedding a fine outer skin and becoming spinners, or imagoes. They then return to the nearby river for mating and are now quite agile fliers, but are still easy to identify by their horizontal body position and their two-winged appearance.

Caddisfly larvae have soft, wormlike bodies with small, weak legs bunched toward the head end. They lack the tough exoskeletons of mayflies and stoneflies, and most live in a self-constructed case of twigs or sand granules. Before hatching, they seal off the end of their case and enter a semidormant pupal state for several days or weeks. When ready to emerge, they bite open the top of the case and swim to the surface, where they split the pupal skin and hatch quite rapidly. The adult is easily identified at rest because it folds its wings horizontally over the body in an inverted V. Caddis in flight show broad, opaque wings, no tails, long antennae—and look very much like small moths. They fly strongly but rather erratically, changing direction suddenly and sharply, though they usually move in an upstream direction.

From even these capsulized descriptions, the average fisherman should be able to identify at a glance ninety percent of the insects he sees on the stream. Yet it's amazing how few anglers bother with this simple diagnosis. Most swarms of caddisflies are shrugged off as "brush hatches"—meaning that all the flies are coming out of the bushes instead of off the water and therefore the trout are feeding on some other insect. Many of the insects may, indeed, be coming from the bushes, for caddis may live for several weeks as adults and return to the river each evening for mating or egg-laying. But that's no reason for crossing them off. Very likely some of the same species are hatching out that evening and many of the previously hatched flies will be buzzing the surface enticingly.

The other main reason caddisflies are ignored is that their coverage in trout-fishing books has been skimpy, to put it mildly. True, there is usually some useful information on fishing imitations of the emerging pupae in fast or streamy water, and the excellent Ed Sens' pupal imitations represent one of the very few attempts to deal seriously with the caddis in any form. Dry-fly imitation of the adult caddis is usually dismissed because, first, caddis are seen more in the air than on the water and are, therefore, seldom available to trout, and, second, most caddis hatch after dark when fishermen have gone home.

Unfortunately, there's just enough truth in both of these observations to have discouraged serious experimentation so far. But do they really stand up under close scrutiny? Aren't mayflies also noticed more readily when flying than when floating quietly downstream? And don't most mayflies hatch in late evening—or at night—once the blustery days of early spring are over?

There are some more positive arguments in favor of trying to imitate the adult caddis. First, caddisflies are enormously profuse. Dr. Cornelius Betten, a leading entomologist of his day, said that five hundred and sixty-eight separate caddis species had been identified in North America alone. And since most of the work he referred to had been completed before 1910, the final figure will obviously be very much higher. Second, caddis lead much longer adult lives than mayflies—weeks instead of days. As a result, trout get many more potential tries at every individual insect as it returns to the river each evening. Third, adult caddis are available over a longer season than are mayflies. I have seen them hatching as late in the year as December and as early as February—nearly two months before and after mayflies can be expected. The correct presentation of good caddis imitations can therefore lengthen a dry-fly addict's trout season well into the fall. Fourth, caddisflies seem to be especially delicious to trout. While some species of mayflies are rarely taken by trout and some stoneflies are avoided by them, I have never noticed a species of caddis that wasn't eaten with relish. Fifth, and most important, some of the largest hatches of flies I have ever seen have been caddis hatches and some of the wildest surface feeding I have ever witnessed has been to these same caddis hatches.

After reviewing much of the above evidence in my mind several years ago, I came to the startling conclusion that perhaps the caddis dry-fly enigma was one of the last big fly-fishing frontiers. Although I realized I was far from the best-qualified person to take on this mission, I did feel that my discovery of the frontier itself gave me some rights of exploration. I began by rummaging around in the untidy attic of memory where past fishing experiences are stored. I quickly recalled my complete failure during the great hatch on the Beaverkill, which I recounted earlier, and a number of very similar experiences as well. But they merely reinforced what most fishing authorities had already said: Dry-fly fishing (or at least conventional dry-fly fishing) was seldom effective during a caddis hatch. My Adirondack experience, on the other hand, held out some hope for the surface-fished fly under these conditions. For the nineteenth-century dancing dropper had been very deadly indeed when trout were gorging on caddis. Here, at least, was a solid starting point.

I dug out my longest trout rod, an eight-and-a-half-footer, and matched it with my lightest fly line. I then tied up a level leader with two dropper attachments. This improvised rig was no joy to cast with, but I found I could cover fast-flowing pocket water with it quite effectively when I worked in a downstream direction. In fact, I discovered that this technique was not only more productive than the upstream dry fly in this kind of water, but that it was more exciting, too. Fish slashed at the dropper viciously, sometimes coming completely out of water on the strike. And when I remembered to wobble the rod tip and zigzag the dropper over one of these miniature, bubble-filled pools, results showed even further improvement. The tail fly may have hung dead in the current, but the top dropper bounced from side to side over the surface in a highly appetizing manner.

However, when I came to the end of the rapids where the water fanned out and flattened into a pool, I met defeat again. There simply wasn't enough current to pull the line and the flies far enough away from me. Fish could see much farther in this calm water, too. I was spooking every trout I approached long before I could dance my tantalizing fly over his head. So, while I had added an exciting and effective technique to my fast-water strategy, I had not begun to solve the main problem. It was in the slow water of the pools and flats where the real challenge lay. Here the sunk pupal imitations, the skittered wet fly, and the conventional dry fly had all failed time and time again. And it was precisely here that so many caddis hatched out and that I had seen so many plump, deliberate trout pluck the fluttering adults from the surface!

One tempting solution I had read about years ago had been worked out by English poachers in an earlier and more caddis-oriented era. Two fishermen would position themselves on opposite sides of a slow but productive stretch of water after having tied their leaders together. They would then advance very slowly upstream, holding their rods high so that only their dropper flies tickled the surface out in midstream. When a fish struck—and this must have been fairly frequently—one fisherman let out line while the other reeled the fish in. The technique was quickly outlawed, and I believe rightly so, but you have to admire the ingenuity of it. Like the old stillwater dropper technique, the poachers' dap recreated the telltale motions of an adult caddis bouncing over the water's surface.

It was just this characteristic caddis motion I'd found I couldn't duplicate legally or practically on flat water. But perhaps there was some other quickly recognizable caddis behavior pattern that I could imitate effectively. I resolved to spend less time fishing and more time observing in the future. Like all good resolutions, this one was easier promised than kept. For the most rewarding observations must always be made when flies are most numerous and fish are feeding. Yet, despite notable lapses, my research eventually yielded two bits of simple but little-discussed information. First, evening flights of returning caddis invariably took an upstream direction. Very likely this is nature's way of assuring continuing populations in the headwaters since so many lumbering caddis larvae must be washed downstream during spates. Whatever the reason, this characteristic is very pronounced and, as we shall see, significant. Second, both hatching caddis and the ones alighting on the surface for egg-laying seemed to exhibit the same behavior pattern. They would float a few feet, then make a short, erratic lurch upcurrent—repeating this at intervals as long as they remained on the water. While this characteristic seemed far less dramatic than the zigzag flight pattern in the air, perhaps it would be equally distinctive to trout. After all, a fly actually on the water must be worth a dozen in the air.

I decided to put this hypothesis to the test during a vacation in mid-June when the dark blue caddis hatch was in full swing. This fly, scientifically named *Psilotreta frontalis,* is perhaps the single most abundant and important insect on the river I fish regularly. It begins hatching about Memorial Day and is seen in large numbers for an hour or more every clement evening until well into July. On cold, blustery days, it either appears earlier in the afternoon or makes no appearance at all. Unless I am mistaken, this is the caddis species that had baffled me on the Beaverkill many years before. I decided to devote every evening for two weeks to settling this old score— whether I caught any fish or not. My hope was that the short, sudden motion of the fly in an upstream direction would convince the trout that my fly was indeed a caddisfly.

I started out by tying some flies on light #16 hooks with dun tails, dun bodies, and longish dun hackles. Not an exact imitation, by a long shot, but it did give the impression of a blue caddis with its wings extended and it had taken fish fairly well in fast, choppy water. Most important, it floated high and would tend to skitter instead of sinking when I twitched it. Casting this fly upstream and across in the usual dry-fly manner was, as I had expected, no good at all. When I twitched the fly from this position, it moved faster than the current and usually put a rising fish down. Fishing straight across stream worked a bit better, but I still wasn't raising a very high percentage of the fish I'd spotted. Across and downstream? Heresy or no, I gave it a try and the action picked up immediately. Later on, purely by accident, I threw a pronounced curve cast. This time when I imparted the minute twitch to the line, the fly moved a sudden inch straight upstream. Then, as it dropped back into a dead drift, it disappeared into the mouth of the best trout of the evening.

I thought I had it solved then and there. Cast across and a bit downstream with a good curve, landing the fly three feet or so above a noticed rise. Twitch the fly slightly upstream the instant it touches the water—before line or leader can start to sink. Then give it slack to float drag-free as far as possible. I was close, tantalizingly close, to the solution. In fact, everything was right—except the fly. In that clear, calm water, the silhouette just wasn't enough like a caddis. I was having a heyday with the small fish, but I wasn't fooling many of the better class of trout. And this was very significant.

Sad as it may seem, all trout are not created equal. Rainbow trout, at least in our eastern streams, are acrobatic but not very selective. Native brook trout, when they're really on the feed, will take almost anything. Freshly stocked trout of any variety tend to be pleasantly gullible. Wild brown trout, however, seldom make mistakes once they've grown up. When you're getting refusals from browns weighing more than a pound you can be sure you're not fooling them.

Clearly, what I needed was a dry-fly imitation of the adult caddis that could stand the scrutiny of wary brown trout in glassy water. The most likely prototypes I could find were the English "sedges" which are still being tied in Halford's style. These flies are tailless, have hackle at the head, and longish wings of primary wing feathers lying back over the body. I tied up several blue caddis on this model, making sure that the wings were parallel to the body, covering it like an inverted boat. This new fly looked very promising when I made a trial cast with it the following evening. The inverted V of the wings trapped a sizable air bubble and the fly rode the water in the precise position of the natural. It looked just like the real thing. But when I started fishing it across and down with my new technique, a fatal flaw appeared. It just couldn't stand up to the rigors of the indispensable twitch. This small but decisive movement dislodged the air bubble and left the fly floating tail down.

But I was on the right track. On those few occasions when the fly didn't end up half-submerged, trout—good trout—took it with confidence. I fished out the rest of the hatch that season with this imitation, working on my execution of the twitch to the point where I could bring it off about twenty percent of the time. It made for exacting fishing, but results were far better than before.

The problem kept bothering me, though. That winter, as I sat at my vise tying up next season's supply, my thoughts kept returning to the caddis. I realized that I needed more floating power over the bend of the hook where some two-thirds of the metal lies and where there is the least amount of material that can take advantage of surface tension. Winding hackle the length of the body, as Halford had done in some cases, was tempting and logical. But it didn't work. There was some gain in floating power, but the bristle of hackle made the wing ride unrealistically high above the body. Fore-and-aft construction—that is, with a hackle at the bend as well as at the head—caused the same winging problem and looked even less like the actual insect. After hours of frustration, I finally resorted to brute logic in an attempt to prove to myself that I had gone about as far as I could go. The desperate syllogism went something like this: The bend of the hook needs the most flotation. Steely spade hackles from the throat of a fighting cock are the best-floating, most water-repellent feathers. Ergo: I must make the wing of spade hackle fibers. There was one hitch to this plan, though. Spade hackles are as scarce as the proverbial hen's teeth. Some otherwise superb hackle necks don't have any of these feathers at all. A very few necks may produce a dozen or so. In any event, these precious feathers must be hoarded for the tails of mayfly duns, as good flotation is a critical problem with these flies, too.

After a lot of thought and a little tying, I came up with what I considered a likely looking prototype. By keeping the body extremely thin, I found I could tie in the spade hackle fibers so that they would lie nearly parallel to the hook shank. Then, by positioning small bunches along both sides of the hook shank and on up over the top, distributing the fibers evenly, an extremely realistic caddis wing resulted. Finished off with two good hackles at the head, it looked every bit as good as the Halford-type caddis when I floated them side by side in the bathroom sink.

The next spring was a long time coming (as it always seems to be), but finally I was on the river in mid-May during a strong hatch of shad fly. And for once abstract theory triumphed! The new fly floated perfectly even after it had been twitched, for the wing itself, which was almost twice as long as the body, acted as the floatingest tail a fly ever had. The silhouette proved every bit as killing as the Halford-winged fly. And, as a bonus, the fly proved to be nearly indestructible, an unexpected but major blessing since each fly had enough spade hackle in its wing to tail more than a dozen standard duns!

One thing about this fly puzzled me for years, though: the manner in which trout take it. They rise to it deliberately, even boldly, yet seldom exhibit the hurried slash that usually greets the dapped dropper fly. I am now satisfied that the reason for this different type of rise is the fact that more caddis are injured in hatching from the pupal sheath than casual observation would indicate. We see the many defective mayflies floating down the pool because their erect wings advertise their helplessness. The low-slung, injured caddis often escapes the angler's eye—though not the trout's. And I believe the same is true of caddis that have returned to the river and die on the surface. In any event, the fish seem well acquainted with the caddis as a sitting duck once it has identified itself with that characteristic upstream lurch.

What sizes and colors of this fly should an angler carry? A definitive answer is virtually impossible. The closer the fly is to the natural the better, and every river I've fished seems to be different. For example, of the four caddis species that hatch most profusely on the river I fish each year, two are quite unimportant on another river of similar size less than twenty miles away. However, the great majority of stream-bred caddis range between hook size #16 and #12.

Most are somber-hued, running to gingers, browns, grays, and duns. For best results, you'll have to observe, collect, and experiment on your own rivers. If you don't tie, take specimens of the most abundant species to a friend who does, or to a professional. Caddis are tough and may live for several days in captivity.

I can recommend the special construction of this fly and the twitch-method of fishing it without any reservation when caddis are hatching or buzzing over the water. After several years of this type of fishing, I can honestly say that *I am now more confident of taking a good trout rising in flat water when the caddis is on than I am when fishing a standard dun during a mayfly hatch.*

This strong preference for fishing a caddisfly hatch dates from a memorable evening a few years ago and has been reinforced many times since then. A friend had invited me to fish with him on an especially interesting piece of water. The home pool on this stretch had been Theodore Gordon's favorite, according to Gordon's former fishing companion, Herman Christian. More recently, Hewitt had fished here regularly for decades and La Branche was often with him. Stepping into this water is like walking into Westminster Abbey. A piece of bad luck delayed me and I didn't arrive till nearly dusk. This was especially unfortunate, since it was the last weekend of the season and these would be my last casts for more than six months. As I joined my host at the head of the long, curving pool, I was further discouraged by his report on conditions. "It's pretty dead. A few flies in the air, but none hatching. The only real action I've seen was down under that overhanging hemlock." He pointed across and well downstream. "Several good ones rising there, but I couldn't get a touch out of them. I'll work the choppy water up here. Why don't you go down and give them a go? It'll be dark in twenty minutes, anyway."

I walked down the bank and watched for a minute or two. I marked down six trout under the tree and all were rising regularly. The flies in the air were definitely caddis and a species I had met before. I tied on a #16 ginger-colored imitation and went to work on the lowest fish. I will resist the temptation to file a cast-by-cast report on the subsequent fifteen minutes, but I do want to mention the final score: One fish raised and pricked; two hooked that finally kicked off; two wild yellow-bellied browns between twelve and fourteen inches landed and released. The sixth fish? I'm sure I sent him scurrying while playing number five, which ran strongly upstream. A very respectable record for minutes of fishing behind one of the best anglers I know.

I couldn't help wondering what Gordon, Hewitt, and La Branche would have thought of my strange-looking fly and the way that I'd twitched it. Would they have disregarded it as they had the dropper-fly technique—or would they have thought it a stumbling step forward?

1970

10

A Dry-Fly Philosophy

Forget the dry-fly color you see.
Under some light conditions trout
perceive something quite different.

Socrates gave his wife all the credit for his success as a philoso-
pher, but not in the usual I-owe-it-all-to-the-little-lady sense. He
claimed Xanthippe was such a shrew and all-around five-letter girl
that she had driven him into the arms of abstract thought.

I think Socrates was putting us on, though. If his theory held
water, sheer frustration would also drive dry-fly fishermen to
embrace pure logic and, as a result, they would surely quit fishing.
Instead, they head for the stream at every opportunity armed with
new flies, new theories, and new hopes even though sad experience
has proved that for every small sip of success there are many cup-
fuls of hemlock to be choked down. I always get depressed by the
top-heavy failure/success ratio when I reread my own fishing diary,
and the disastrous day of July 5, 1964, is a typical example.

The previous evening had set me up for the coming defeat. In the hour before pitch darkness I had raised, pricked, or caught every rising fish I had cast to with a new imitation of a pale-yellowish dun that had long been one of the most baffling hatches on my river. I was especially pleased with this performance because the sudden-death imitation had been created in the classic manner—duplicated from live, captured specimens. I won't go into the whole dressing, for reasons that will soon become obvious, but the major change I had made from previous recipes was in the body, where I had substituted porcupine hair dyed the color of creamery butter for the usual, much duller fox-belly fur. With this inspired concoction I had given a dozen and a half trout a good toothache before darkness and a sudden downpour had driven me from the river.

By the next day, the infamous 5th of July, the river had risen six inches and, since it was still drizzling, I spent most of the morning tying up a boxful of my new "Yellow Perils." The sun came out at two o'clock and by four I was on the river—playing a hunch that cooling rainwater might start the flies hatching several hours early.

Again, my touch was pure magic. At four-thirty the same pale yellow duns started pouring down my favorite flat and despite the bright sunlight the trout came strongly on the feed. This was going to be ridiculously easy. Higher, faster water would make the fish far less shy and I had a whole boxful of my new secret weapons. I fully expected to walk away within an hour, fed up with fishing that was too murderous to be fun.

As it turned out, it was more than three hours later when I finally left the river and my hands hardly smelled fishy. I had caught only two six-inchers and had been totally ignored by all the fish old enough to spawn. What had gone wrong? How could trout have savaged an imitation one evening then acted like militant consumerists when presented with the identical fly the very next day? The higher water, which had actually relieved near-drought conditions, should have been strongly in my favor. The critical difference appeared to be available light—heavily clouded skies at dusk versus bright afternoon sun.

Up to that point, I had thought of light as a basic commodity that could be measured on a simple scale of more or less. After all, an artificial fly in the hand looks much the same to us at dusk as it does in sunlight except for the brightness of the colors. This is true, however, only because we tend to view it in terms of the light it reflects back to our eyes.

Unfortunately, the trout's world and his modes of perception are quite different and far more complicated. He sees a mayfly floating overhead in at least three distinct ways and in many combinations of the three. In extremely poor light the fly probably blocks out all the rays reaching the trout's eyes and appears as a colorless silhouette. In bright sunlight the same insect seems mainly translucent, the light passing through the body, wings, and legs with only slight refraction, and the color of its internal organs may be even more distinctive than the color of its skin. Then, of course, when perceived by reflected light, the fly may look to the trout much as it does to us, but I believe this is only for relatively short periods of time between the translucent and opaque light conditions.

I think this explains my ups and downs on the July 4th and 5th I mentioned earlier. The imitation fooled the fish at dusk because it was being seen by reflected light at first, perhaps, and then as a pure silhouette. However, this same artificial had none of the translucence of the natural when viewed against the bright sky the following day and may well have been passed up as an inedible hemlock needle.

If you hold a live mayfly between your eye and a bright light, then at a right angle to the light and finally against a very dim light, your eye may well convince you that you have been looking at three separate insects, and if you move the fly slowly through all three stages you may see an almost infinite number of gradations in the appearance of that same fly. This nearly duplicates what a trout probably sees during the various hours of a single day and when you consider this enormous variety of perceptions, you may easily, and rightly, despair of ever creating, or finding, the perfect artificial of any insect.

What we often tend to forget is that all dry flies are a compromise between the true appearance of a natural insect and what we can manage to spin on a relatively heavy hook and then float over a fish. Each type, or even tying, of an artificial is based on the premise that some of the things a trout perceives are more important than others in convincing him that this is lean red meat and not just a bundle of fluff. These aspects are emphasized while others, deemed less important, are necessarily sacrificed. With this in mind, let's look at some of the most popular schools of dry-fly tying, restricting our scrutiny to mayfly artificials since, for some inscrutable reason, 99 percent of all floaters sold imitate this form of aquatic insect.

To make things simpler, let's break flies down into their four basic parts: tail, body, hackle, and wing. I'm sure trout don't do this, but fly tyers do and this piece-by-piece approach helps put some order into centuries of fly-tying chaos.

Tails are the least controversial and worried-over part of the classic dry fly. Many of the most effective wet flies omit them altogether so it's easy to conclude that these hairlike and unnourishing appendages aren't the focal point of the trout's attention. The earliest dry flies on record sported only two or three whisks—exactly the number of tails (or *setae*) the naturals themselves possess. However, this number was soon increased for practical reasons and, since trout apparently can't count, the more fully fibered tails are the norm today.

Don't let this mislead you into thinking that tails are just so much excess baggage, though. These few fibers are called upon to support and float nearly two-thirds of the total hook-weight—the heaviest portion over the bend and barb—and a short, sparse tail can condemn the rear end of a floater to sink below the surface film and leave your imitation pitched at an improbable angle. To prevent this, I tie my flies with the tail fibers splayed out in a horizontal fan, spreading 30 to 40 degrees, the way most naturals flair their tails. I have no great faith that trout appreciate this small gesture toward realism, but this does help prevent tail-sinking and it has other advantages, too. This fanned-out position offers much more air resistance and helps the imitation flutter down to the surface in the horizontal plane we hope for. And, since the fibers are spread out perpendicular to the hook-bend, it helps to cock the fly in a bolt-upright position once it hits the water.

Many years ago I showed one of our most famous fly tyers a series I had tied up in this manner, asking his professional appraisal. "Sure it floats a fly better, and presents it better, too. We've known that for years," he added, dashing my hopes for immortality as the Thomas Edison of fly tying. "But they'd never sell. People expect flies to have a straight, bunched tail and that's what they get." He was right, of course. I have since seen fan-tailed flies illustrated in books and articles, but I have never seen them offered in tackle shops. However, I think it will pay you to tie up some flies like this or get a friend to create some for you. They're that much better.

When we come to fly bodies we enter the eye of a storm that has been raging for centuries. The first dry flies had spun-fur bodies as did the ancient wet patterns described by Charles Cotton in *The Compleat Angler.* Nearly ninety years ago, Frederick M. Halford, the English genius who launched and popularized the dry fly, decided that these fuzzy-bodied imitations weren't realistic enough—at least not from a photographic point of view. In line with his doctrine of "exact imitation" he redesigned these flies with glistening, segmented bodies of horsehair dyed to a precise color. Although these same patterns are sold and used on Britain's chalk-streams to this day, the pendulum has swung back toward the older style in recent years and you now have a wide choice of body-types in even shop-tied flies.

One of the more interesting rebuttals to Halford's hard-nosed theory was launched by an English mathematician in 1924. J. W. Dunne, along with many fellow dry-fly fishers, had long felt that Halford's patterns, though ultrarealistic when viewed under side-lighted conditions, were opaque and lifeless when seen against a strong light. Dunne's "Sunshine" flies were designed with bodies made of a special synthetic fiber wound over a white-painted hook-shank. When these flies were dipped into a flask of special "Sunshine" oil, they suddenly took on both the color and transparency of the naturals.

"Sunshine" flies have not been on the market since World War II, as far as I can tell, but they may have been a giant step in the right direction. Their disappearance from the catalogs was not due to their lack of killing properties, though. Like so many other demonstrably better flies both before and since, they were just too difficult and time-consuming to tie. And the synthetic body material was extremely fragile. One sharp trout-tooth could unravel and ruin the laboriously created body.

Hard bodies of quill, stiff hair, and other opaque materials are still popular. But many tyers have taken the cue from Dunne and developed translucent bodies of simpler, tougher materials. The old fur-dubbings, particularly those spun from the underfur of aquatic mammals, are reasonably water-repellant, show a lifelike sparkle, and allow enough light to refract through their fuzzy margins to give some hint of transparency. Seal's fur is probably the best of all since it has the most lustre and changes color least when wet. This type of body has gained popularity in recent years and so have those made of fine herls, which also give a translucent appearance.

In selecting bodies of this sort it is best to hold them up to the light (preferably when wet) to choose the shade you hope the fish will see. Over three hundred years ago, Charles Cotton pointed out that the only way to tell a fur dubbing's true color was to hold it up to a strong light. It seems to take a discouragingly long time to rediscover what was common knowledge years ago.

There is one situation in which hard, slim quill bodies may be a better choice, though, and that's when imitating the mayfly spinners that fall spent on the surface at dusk. This second, and less important, stage of the mayfly's flying life has a characteristically thinner body than the earlier dun stage, and since it is usually viewed against the fading light of late evening, a slim body of durable quill or hair may present a more realistic silhouette. You can usually discount the factor of translucence under such light conditions. Remember Gilbert and Sullivan's description of the rich attorney's elderly ugly daughter? "She'd well pass for forty-three in the dusk with the light behind her." You, too, can probably fool a poor fish under these flattering conditions, but I doubt that you'd want to be wed to that style of tying for the harsh, unforgiving light of midday.

Hackle is the most important part of any dry fly as far as keeping it afloat is concerned. In classic theory, it is supposed to represent the legs of the insect, but that isn't necessarily the case in modern practice. Spiders, variants, bivisibles, and conventional wingless patterns use hackle to represent both legs and wings and so, in part, do some of the most famous Catskill patterns like the Quill Gordon and the Hendrickson. The wings of bunched wood-duck fibers in these popular patterns are not at all the color of the mayflies' wings they are supposed to imitate. These barred yellow feathers are used to represent the venation of the wings, and their true gray color is recreated only when they are viewed through many turns of dun hackle.

All-hackle flies are popular because they are tough and are high floaters. This latter quality makes them ideal for prospecting in fast runs or in swirling pockets, but I find they're only so-so on the glassy surfaces of pools or flats. Here trout often drift back under a fly for quite a ways before taking it, and these more stylized patterns are often rejected when studied by good-sized, heavily fished trout.

An interesting attempt at creating a high-floating yet realistic imitation was launched by an Englishman, Dr. Baigent, in the early part of this century. The good doctor must have had a bit of the advertising man in him since he named them "Refractra" flies. They looked much like the standard British dressings of his day with this difference: Only one short hackle was used to represent the legs while a second hackle, two or three times as long in the fiber and of a neutral shade, was wound over this, giving a high-floating fly without the usual appearance of too much bulk.

According to Baigent, they had another great advantage. The long, nearly invisible overhackle produced dimples in the surface tension over a wider area, creating extra distortion and refraction so that even the most sophisticated trout couldn't get a sharp look at the fly.

The concept of these flies, like Dunne's "Sunshine" theory, is excellent, and the only reason I can imagine for their disappearance from our inventories is the scarcity of the good-quality, pale-dun hackle needed to create the desired illusion. "Refractra" flies have all the good floating qualities of our standard variants and are far more killing on smooth, slow water. I can only hope that with our accelerated interest in new theories and new patterns that someone will "discover" them again very soon.

Believers in all-hackle flies are convinced that no artificial can fool a trout when it can be seen clearly and that it is mainly the sparkles and dimples set up in the surface tension by the hackle points, creating much the same patterns made by an insect's legs, that deceive the fish. There's considerable evidence to support this premise. Until an artificial enters a trout's relatively small window or direct, above-surface vision, these twinkles in the mirrorlike water surface give the fish his only advance warning of approaching food. This stimulus seems sufficient in fast or turbulent water where trout are forced into making a hair-trigger decision but, in my experience, it leaves something to be desired when the water is slow and slick.

Vincent Marinaro, of Pennsylvania's limestone country, has come up with an ingenious compromise: a type of fly that should produce a more realistic light pattern outside the trout's window yet one that also deceives when viewed directly by the trout. He accomplishes this by splaying the hackle toward the head and tail of the fly when winding it on. This gives the fly two other advantages: more area of surface tension for the hackle to work on and a more accurate representation of the natural fly's spraddled legs.

I don't know why this style of hackling hasn't caught on. Is it because it looks untidy? After all, one of the hallmarks of a well-tied conventional fly is the close, even turn of hackle at the head, and from this criterion Marinaro's tie looks like a botched job. Whether or not this type of hackling offends your esthetic sensibilities, I can assure you that the result is extremely killing—especially in sizes #16 and smaller.

Parachute flies, those with their hackle wound in a horizontal rather than vertical plane, have been on and off the market for over forty years. They, too, spread their hackle over a larger part of the surface the way a mayfly splays its legs. However, they have one distinct drawback. With the hackle wound above the body, as is customary, the body is presented below the surface film, which is uncharacteristic of mayflies. It seems a case of win one, lose one, here.

Flies without any hackle at all have reappeared after a number of years and they certainly deserve a long, hard look. One of the most popular and effective British flies of all time, the Gold-ribbed Hare's Ear, has always been tied in this manner, relying on a few picked-out guard hairs for flotation. This fly is still considered the best dry imitation of the Medium Olive Dun—one of the most important spring flies on England's legendary chalkstreams.

No-hackle flies are unquestionably accurate and deadly imitations under the conditions they were designed for. On English chalkstreams, where this tie originated, most naturals are quite small, averaging to sizes #16 and #18, and artificials of this size are quite easy to float with a minimal grip on surface tension. The water is glassy smooth, and few presentations are made since only rising fish are cast to. Unfortunately, we have very few rivers in this country with similar conditions and opportunities. Where these do exist, no-hackle flies are superb. However, on our usual, more turbulent waters where steady casting and prospecting for unseen fish is standard practice, these flies won't float long enough or high enough to be practical.

Imitations of spinners, or spent mayflies, are a different matter, of course. These are traditionally fished to rising trout at dusk on glassy water, and we want them to float flush in the surface film. The best of these imitations have always been tied without conventional hackle. The easiest and most effective tie, I've found, is made by winding on one hackle, then clipping off all the top and bottom fibers, but you can produce this same, spent-wing effect in many other ways.

Some sort of wing is usually preferred by anglers who concentrate on slow, clear waters, and these upright "sails" of the mayfly dun can be represented in three basic ways. The classic method is with matching slips of primary feathers. A more impressionistic style is created by using split bunches of plumage as many Catskill flies do or by tying in stiff fibers of hair as in the popular Wulff flies. A relatively new school advocates wings formed of whole hackle feathers clipped to a precise mayfly-wing shape.

Using winged flies for slow-water conditions is sound practice. The top of the wing is the first part of a mayfly that a trout can see directly as it starts to enter his window of direct vision. In slow water this preview of the approaching fly may well be the stimulus that starts a fish gliding up to the surface.

Slips of primary quill, from dark to palest dun, will duplicate the wing-color of most flies you'll encounter. On small flies—size #16 and under—these wings are extremely realistic, and they are highly visible to both the trout and the angler. This latter advantage is not to be taken lightly when you're trying to keep track of a #18 fly forty or more feet distant on the surface. Many anglers complain that these quill wings are too fragile and that they break up after a fish or two, but if they have been tied on properly (which, admittedly, is not always the case) the parted fibers can usually be zipped back into a solid wing in seconds.

Medium-sized flies (#16s, #14s, and #12s) are logical candidates for clipped-hackle wings. In sizes smaller than these such wings probably represent a lot of hard work that will be appreciated only by the angler. In fact, these wings are so time-consuming to prepare in all sizes that few professional tyers can afford to offer them. On the positive side, they are realistically translucent, tough, and in larger sizes they are less likely than quill slips to wind up your tippet while casting.

Flies larger than size #12 are probably best tied with bunched-fiber or hair wings. These are less lifelike, of course, but

they are also less rigid. Even clipped-hackle wings over a certain size tend to hum and whirr during high-velocity casting, and they may then wind up your tippet like the rubber band in a model airplane. The largest mayflies—the Green Drake, the March Brown, and others—are the hardest naturals to imitate successfully, and I feel that winging realistically is only a small part of the problem. Trout act as if they see larger objects in a different manner than they see smaller ones. Their eyes seem able to pick big flies to pieces, and even the most realistic imitations of the larger naturals are taken with regularity only in fast water or when trout are on a feeding spree.

This phenomenon is hard to explain, but is attested to by the century-long struggle of Britain's most gifted theorists and fly tyers to come up with an effective imitation of their large Green Drake, usually referred to as *the* Mayfly. There are hundreds of different dressings on the market and yet none of them is considered a reliable killer. In my experience, we have the same problem with our largest insects. This difficulty in deceiving trout with larger floating patterns is so pronounced that I doubt that dry-fly fishing would be at all popular if the average aquatic insect were size #8 or #10 instead of size #14 or #16.

When these giants of the insect world are being taken regularly in slow water (where, unfortunately, most of them hatch out) I usually abandon my faith in the sleight of hand of fly tying. I then put on a higher-floating, but less realistic, variant of similar size and color and give it a slight twitch in an across or upstream direction just before it passes over the rising fish. Easy does it here: just a wiggle. This minimotion, I've found, is often more effective in convincing the trout that your artificial is a living insect than the most inspired fly-tying efforts.

Many years ago, when I first started tying flies, I dreamed I might someday invent a pattern that no trout could resist. A little experience put an end to that fantasy, but soon another one popped up in its place. Why couldn't I design a floating imitation or, say, the March Brown dun that no fish feeding on the naturals would ever refuse?

My fly box bears witness that I have now given up even this more modest ambition. These days I tie up several imitations of the more common mayflies I expect to see during the daylight hours on the waters I fish. To stay with the March Brown, for example, I now carry some long-hackled variant imitations for fast water or to twitch slightly on flat water when all else fails. I have some standard Art Flick imitations with yellowish-cream bodies that work well most of the time. But some days, when the overhead light is especially bright, I do far better with this same dressing tied with a body of rusty-orange seal's fur that suggests the gut color of the natural instead of its yellow skin color. And yet, even with this battery, I sometimes do so poorly during a good March Brown hatch that I'm convinced I'm still missing a trick—or several.

One reason for this is that light conditions vary widely and constantly. Then, too, entomologists tell us that the aquatic insects themselves change color gradually and continually after they've hatched out. And mayflies of the very same species differ considerably in color—and in size—from one river to another even though they may be hatching out in the same ecological region. The more I learn about insects, flies, and fly tying, the more certain I become that the one perfect imitation can never exist.

All this conspires to make fly tying an absorbing occupation of trial and error punctuated by occasional, temporary successes. Many flies, especially those that hatch out during the bright hours of the day, seem to call for several distinct patterns. Larger specimens continue to defy predictable results with any or all imitations. And so far we've only looked into the problems of duplicating adult mayflies. Floating caddisflies, stoneflies, midges, and terrestrials have their own sets of problems. And then there's another universe of nymphs, wetflies, streamers, bucktails, and the other subsurface imitations to look into.

Obviously, trout aren't as gullible as people. You can't fool all of the fish some of the time or even some of the fish all of the time. If you can manage to fool some of the fish some of the time you'll probably be accused of being an expert. Decades of trial and error have forced me to accept this philosophy. It may have helped me *understand* dry-fly problems, but it hasn't helped me *solve* too many of them.

However, from all reports, philosophy didn't help Socrates solve his problems, either. To begin with, he was extremely ugly. After he married, his wife tried to make his life a hell on earth. And when the citizens of Athens told him to drop dead, they meant it literally. Things might have been worse, though. Think of the added grief he'd have gone through if he'd been addicted to dry-fly fishing.

1975

11

The All-American Fly

The wet fly, dry fly, and nymph
all originated across the pond.
But the streamer is ours, all ours!

While the dry fly, nymph, and winged wet fly were pirated from the other side of the Atlantic, the streamer fly was born in the U.S.A. and is ours, all ours. It's as American as a slice of Mom's apple pie with a scoop of vanilla on top.

Unfortunately, there's no consensus on who invented this fly or exactly when. I like to believe the story that a standard wet fly's hackle became unwound one day and, with the feathers trailing out behind, caught fish after fish—but that incident is probably apocryphal.

We do know, however, that this minnow-imitating fly and its more recent cousin, the bucktail, first became popular on the land-locked salmon and squaretail fisheries of northern Maine around the turn of the century and then spread to other parts of the country. We also know that Herb Welch and Carrie Stevens played major roles in creating the first, and still popular, patterns.

Why streamer/bucktail fishing has never caught on in Europe puzzles me. A couple of decades ago, I fished for two weeks on Austria's fabled Traun River where low, industrial dams created chutes of deep, fast water.

"Here are big trout," my guide informed me. "You must put on heavy leader and salmon fly." He held out a fully-dressed, 1/0 Silver Doctor. I shook my head and pulled out my fleece-lined book of streamers. I picked out a three-and-a-half-inch, landlocked-salmon-sized Grey Ghost and tied it on. The guide's eyes bulged. He'd never seen a fly that looked anything like that before.

Neither had the Traun trout. I hooked nearly a dozen fish in the 4- to 8-pound category during the next hour, though I lost half of them when they managed to snag me in a small tree that had become lodged under the dam. Finally, the guide, who was also a local fisheries officer, made me reel in on the charge that I was brutalizing too many trout.

When I left, I gave the *Fischmeister* my remaining supply of streamers plus all the long-shank hooks in my fly-tying kit. I felt he was going to ask the mayor of the small, nearby city of Gmunden to rename the town in my honor.

Equally puzzling to me, for years, was why it took so long to come up with a fly that looked and acted like a baitfish. After all, artificial flies are at least 1,700 years old and fishermen knew, centuries before that, that big fish ate little ones.

Only recently, have I come up with what I think is a plausible explanation for this. Insect-imitating flies weren't invented as an affectation. They were simply a practical solution to a vexing problem. When fish were seen feeding on mayflies or caddisflies, the angler couldn't just capture a natural and impale it on his hook. If he tried, all he got for his efforts was gooey fingers. Chicken feathers and fur, however, could be turned into a near-enough counterfeit and one that would stay on his hook while casting.

It wasn't until the late-nineteenth century, when the dry-fly craze hit Britain, that anything like "purism" entered the picture. Before that time, if an angler located a big, carnivorous trout, he unabashedly put a live (or dead) minnow on his hook and that was that. It's only since late-Victorian days that fly fishers have felt ashamed to be seen with a minnow bucket or Prince Albert can.

The classic streamer/bucktail is tied on a 3X hook with a wing about twice as long as its body. However, a few patterns, such as the Edson Tigers, Black-nosed Dace, and Muddler Minnow call for noticeably shorter wings.

The standard presentation is to cast the fly across and downstream and, as it arcs downcurrent, make it dart with sharp tugs on the line. On still waters, much the same action is imparted by retrieving line in short twitches. In both instances, you can make your fly travel deeper by adding split shot, using a sinking or sink-tip line, pausing before starting your retrieve, or a combination of all three.

While these flies are usually fished at a slightly brisker pace than the old wet fly, it pays to experiment. Sometimes a much faster retrieve—one that even skitters the fly across the surface—will jump-start a previously blasé fish.

Hooking a fish in fast-water runs and heads of pools—places where I find streamers most effective—is largely a matter of luck. If the fish really wants the fly, he'll usually hook himself. If his take is half-hearted or tentative, you'll probably just feel a tug or a tap and that will be the end of it. When fish are really not on the feed, or your fly is not of an appealing size or color, you'll get more flashes, swirls, and bumps than actual hook-ups.

In stillwater lakes and ponds, however, you'll have a little more control. No matter what the speed of your retrieve, when you feel a hit, don't strike, but continue the same retrieve until you feel the solid throb of the fish. Why this delayed strike is essential in still-water fly fishing escapes me. But

M·C·WEILER

every Down-East guide I've ever fished with swears this is the way to go. I missed so many good fish before I acquired this discipline—as unnatural a reflex as the one of not striking an Atlantic salmon—that I'm now a devout believer.

Streamers and bucktails are usually considered as nearly synonymous yet they do have subtle differences. Feather wings have a slightly faster sink rate and they pulsate a bit more than the stiffer hair wings.

However, these differences are disappearing because the bucktail has been gradually losing its "buck." Since deer-tail hair tends to be stiff, opaque, and poor-sinking because of the air trapped in its hollow fibers, tyers are increasingly turning to alternate materials. Polar bear and crinkly calf tail have a translucent, fleshy look when wet, are more supple, and better sinkers than deer hair. FisHair and other synthetics now available have similar characteristics. Today, the feather versus hair rivalry is pretty much a dead heat.

For generations, anglers have been questioning whether or not fish actually mistake these lures for live minnows. Does a trout slam your Grey Ghost streamer for the same reason that he sucks in your dry Hendrickson during a hatch of naturals? Or is the streamer taken mainly because it represents a healthy mouthful that must be alive and edible since it's moving?

A glance at the color plates of popular flies in tackle catalogs won't help you come up with an answer. Some, like the famous Mickey Finn are simply garish. Others, like Lew Oatman's Brook Trout are attempts at exact imitation right down to the painting of red and yellow spots along its sides.

I, personally, tilt toward the imitation theory and usually tie on a Grey Ghost, Nine Three, or Magog Smelt where I know that the prevalent baitfish are smelt. However, the Black Ghost and Yellow Marabou—neither of which looks anything like any minnow I've ever seen—catch their share of brooks, browns, and landlocks every year. So does the ultrasparse and merely suggestive Deep Clouser Minnow. So many, in fact, that I won't bet any real money on my hunch.

Killing as it has proved to be, the all-American fly does have one serious flaw. Unless your backcast is timed nearly perfectly, its long wing is liable to catch in the bend of the hook—rendering it utterly fishless. When there's an obstacle behind you or a contrary and gusty wind, you have to check your fly every few casts or all you'll get is exercise.

There are solutions to this problem, though. One is to tie on short-winged flies like the Edson Tigers or Muddler Minnow when casting conditions are difficult. Another is to resort to a Matuka-style fly. This import from New Zealand is tied with the first half of the hackle lashed to the hook-shank or to the body with only the lower half trailing behind the bend of the hook. Both the short-wings and the Matuka are nearly foul-free, but they don't have quite as seductive an action as the fully winged streamer.

Perhaps the best option is to tie (or have tied) patterns in two separate sections the way the famous Joe Brooks' "blonde" flies are. If I'm making, say, a Mickey Finn, I tie in sparse, hook-length clumps of yellow, red, then yellow again calf tail at the bend, spiral silver tinsel up the shank, then repeat the yellow-red-yellow as a wing that doesn't quite reach the bend. The result has almost exactly the same look and action as the original, but doesn't need constant checking.

For the first fifty years of its existence, the streamer stayed fairly stable and static. At least two generations of anglers tied on the same time-tested patterns, year after year.

But since World War II, the old rulebook has been rewritten. The explosion in saltwater fly fishing and the attempts to lure stripers, blues, bonefish, barracuda, and, most recently, billfish, have stirred the creative juices in fly tyers. This sea-change has resulted in blondes, Deceivers, Bendbacks, and a host of other new styles in tying. These revolutionary new types, and the synthetics they often use, are trickling back into freshwater flies. It would be rash indeed to try to predict what our most popular lake-and-stream minnow-flies will look like only a decade from now.

For years, fly fishers have been labelled "effete elitists," but I think that's no longer valid. Forget the argument that fly fishing is practical because trout prefer an appropriate dry fly over a worm when there's a hatch of mayflies. The streamer/bucktail is simply a devastating lure for catching large, carnivorous fish.

Admittedly, even a beginner spinfisherman can lob his lure far-ther out across the water than an expert fly caster can, but that's only a small fraction of the game. Spoons, spinners, or ingenious wobbling plugs aren't a match for the streamer; it's just the most seductive replica of a real live bait minnow that the hand of man has been able to contrive.

Baitfish don't wobble, zigzag, or flash like neon signs. Live min-nows appear far more subtle than that. They swim with a slight flutter of their tails, their fins pulsate moderately as they travel, and most of the smallish ones tend to be translucent. All of these are properties represented by streamers and few, or none, apply to solid spinning lures.

A few friends and I frequently fish a spot where a river slows down as it enters a large impoundment. To duck the crowds, we take the much longer hike in and fish this hot spot across-river from the easily accessible shoreline. I can't recall a single instance when our streamers haven't out-caught the spin-fishermen across the way—except, of course, when the trout hadn't pulled up in there and we all drew blank.

Further evidence: The specialists who cast or troll for landlocks, square-tails, and lakers at ice-out on the lakes of northern New England are mainly streamer-fly enthusiasts. Wobbling spoons come in a poor second and then there's all the rest of the lures.

Additionally, there's the case of the state conservation officer who, for half of the year, had the enviable job of catching bass in lakes and ponds for scale samples to check growth rates. He was authorized to use any kind of bait, lure, or net—anything short of dynamite—to capture his samples. He almost always chose the streamer.

A track record like that makes me feel proud to be a citizen of the country that invented and developed this style of tie. So much so, that I'm tempted to create a new red-white-and-blue bucktail to honor this feat. Let's see . . . over the silver body, I'll tie in white hair to imitate a minnow's belly, then red to suggest it's been injured and is an easy mark, then blue on top to represent its dark back. Hey, that's not so bad, is it? In fact, it sounds so good it just might give the murderous Mickey Finn a run for its money!

1993

12

The Unsinkable
Wet Fly

Most modern trouters consider
wet flies Stone Age relics.
How wrong they are.

Most advanced fly fishermen I know seldom fish with wet flies anymore, and the youngest of them don't even carry wet-fly patterns. You don't have to be a research analyst to see that this has all the earmarks of a significant trend and, if it continues, in a few years it will be harder to find a wet fly than a #22 midge hook in a haystack. Today, nearly all sunk-fly fishing is done with nymphs. They've almost completely replaced the small, somber wet flies like the Leadwing Coachman, Hare's-Ear, and Dark Cahill, while the Mickey Finn, Muddler, and Spuddler seem to have shouldered the big, bright wets out of the fly hooks and into the attics where moths can complete their destruction.

This may or may not be a loss to fishermen, but fishing catalogs are certainly poorer because of it. Nothing dressed up a color plate as did the old Scarlet Ibis, Parmachene Belle, Silver Doctor,

Jenny Lind, and their peer group. Even our present-day salmon flies with their plain hair wings seem drab in comparison.

The reason these brilliant wet flies are no longer with us is that the special type of fishing for which they were designed disappeared long before they did. When the brook-trout ponds and lakes of Maine, the Adirondacks, and southern Canada were fished down, these patterns had no further purpose. But in their time and place they were murderous.

By sheer luck I caught the tail end of this fishing many years ago in central New Brunswick, and if I hadn't experienced it myself I wouldn't believe the old-time stories. I had been staying at a salmon camp enjoying rotten fishing, and the operator, worried about the possible departure of his paying guests, came up with a delaying tactic. A new area had just been opened up by logging, he told us, and there was now a rough, but passable, road into an almost unfished lake. One logger who said he had fished there swore he'd had a hit on every cast.

We were not a gullible bunch but we were eight hundred miles from home with nothing better to do, so three of us made the trip in an old pickup truck over a road designed to make osteopaths rich. After we had arrived and were able to walk again we found the crude raft the logger had made and drifted out onto the lake. And for once everything we'd been told by an outfitter was absolutely true.

Very soon, the promised hit on every cast became monotonous, so we started experimenting. Two flies? Doubles. Three flies? Triples. Then the one man who'd stuck with the single fly said excitedly, "Even when I've got a fish on, I'm still getting hits. I'll bet they're striking the leader knots." After he landed the fish he tied a couple of small bare hooks in at the knots of this gut leader and cast out again. He'd guessed right; he landed his first triple.

One thing we all noticed that day was the brighter the fly, the faster the hit and the bigger the trout. One member of the party found a few old Parmachene Belles in his vest and these were the best of all. They accounted for nearly all the big fish—those of a pound or better—while smaller, duller flies caught nothing over ten inches. The reason was simple. The more successful fish, the ones that had grown big, were the fish that won the race to the food, no matter what it looked like, and it paid to advertise your hook to them. Caution and delicate presentation had nothing to do with success on these virgin waters. Here the old bright wet flies on hulking #6 hooks were supreme.

Though these flashy wet flies had lost their effectiveness on most ponds and lakes long before my day, some of the more subdued patterns from the same generation are still worth carrying. The Black Gnat is a fine imitation of a big housefly or black land beetle. The White Miller can't be equaled when white caddis are hatching out on a northern lake. The Grizzly King is a useful imitation of many green-bodied caddisflies, and the Montreal duplicates some of the darker species in this order of insects.

When flies like these were arbitrarily discarded along with the Christmas-tree wilderness flies, the baby may have been thrown out with the bathwater. There's a lot about the shape and style of the old wet fly to recommend it—so much that I'm working on a whole series of flies based on this principle.

The emphasis on more accurate imitation, the very movement that brought in the nymph as a replacement for the old wet fly, is responsible for leading me in this direction. The patterns I've come up with so far are different from the old ones, but more in color than in shape. When more anglers and fly tyers turn their attention to the neglected wet fly I'm sure that even the few classic patterns that have survived the nymphing revolution will be redesigned or replaced.

One of these that is still popular in the East is the wet version of the Quill Gordon, which is carried and used by many who consider themselves exact imitationists. Since many books have told us that this mayfly (*Epeorus pleuralis*) leaves its nymphal shuck on the river floor and ascends through the water to the surface as a winged adult, a wet-fly pattern is the logical choice until, of course, the fish become preoccupied with surface feeding on the fully formed adults. But which wet fly? The Quill Gordon?

This pattern has yellow wings, a black-and-white striped body, and dun-colored legs. The natural fly is distinctly different, with dark dun wings, creamy olive body, and dark-brown mottled legs. The old English Greenwell pattern, with a slight alteration in the body, is the best imitation I've ever seen or tried. I've fished my version of this fly as part of a two-fly team along with the standard Quill Gordon, altering their positions on the leader regularly, and over the past thirteen springs it has outfished the wet Gordon better than two to one.

The real nymph-maniacs prefer the gray-colored Quill Gordon nymph which tackle suppliers are all too eager to sell you. I wonder why this pattern appears in so many catalogs. The nymph never rises to the surface, as we have noted, and it is one of the last nymphs to be dislodged by high water. It is a fast-water dweller with a short, flattened body and will only be swept away when the rock or boulder it's hiding under gets rolled over by the force of a flood. Long before this occurs the trout will have gorged themselves on the less-secure nymphs washed down to them. I doubt that Quill Gordon nymphs ever lose their grip until the river is so high and muddy that any sort of fly fishing is impossible. This may be a useful general pattern, but I don't think trout mistake it for the Quill Gordon nymph.

The Quill Gordon, both the artificial and the natural, is an extremely popular and famous fly that has been observed and studied more than most. But how many other mayflies emerge in the same manner and would be better imitated by a wet-fly pattern than by a nymph? And how many caddisflies and stoneflies are there that share this underwater emerging behavior? Entomology doesn't provide many answers—aquatic insects haven't been given much attention by scientists lately—but my guess is that this type of emergence is a lot more common than we realize. Remember, the wet fly was not invented in America to catch ravenous and overpopulated brook trout.

The silhouette and the style were worked out in England over several centuries to catch sophisticated and finicky brown trout.

There's another part of the life cycle of aquatic insects that is ignored by the angler who limits himself to dry flies and nymphs exclusively. What happens to flies after they die? The great majority of them fall on the water, of course, which explains why fishing with mayfly-spinner imitations is so effective at dusk. But what about the spent flies—mayflies, caddisflies, and stoneflies—that aren't taken in the pool where they fall but get churned underwater in the rapids directly below? Could a dry fly or nymph imitate these soggy, but winged, insects as well as the classic wet fly in some pattern or form? I am fully convinced that many early and successful wet flies were winged with pale starling primary feathers to imitate mayfly spinners that had gone down for the third time and had been swept downriver for the waiting fish.

The much-neglected caddisflies may give us even more reasons to reconsider the old wet fly. Some common species seem to spring fully fledged from the water as if they had escaped from their pupal shucks well below the surface. Have they hatched directly out of their cases on the stream bottom the way the Quill Gordon mayflies do? I'm betting on it. And don't some other species, with their seemingly instantaneous hatch-out on the surface, appear more like winged adults than pupae as they make this hazardous trip? I'm sure this is the case with many common species. And yet all the new patterns of emerging caddis I see in tackle stores and catalogs are slavish imitations of the pupae as they appear when they are hauled dormant from their cases.

Another caddis behavior pattern that recommends a wet-fly imitation is the egg-laying of several species. Did you know that some (we don't know exactly how many) crawl down roots, rocks, twigs, or weedstalks to lay their eggs underwater? When these have deposited their eggs and drift down-current, dying, the wet fly has to be the most killing imitation.

It is interesting to note that fishermen who have witnessed this egg-laying technique say that the mature female insect takes a bubble of air underwater with her and that she appears like a moving drop of silver. Modern fly fishermen who wouldn't be caught dead fishing a wet fly sporting a tag or entire body of tinsel have, perhaps, outsmarted themselves.

There's another reason to reevaluate the old tinsel-bodied wet fly. We know that a bubble of gas develops rapidly under the pupal shuck of caddisflies and under the nymphal skin of mayflies just before they emerge. The gas bubble helps them hatch out. How does this make the insect appear to the trout? Is the exact color of a nymph or pupa—examined hours or days before it heads for the surface—what the trout sees during this critical time when the insects are most available as food? Or is there a very different silver or golden flash caused by this gas bubble in emergers that telegraphs to the trout that this is their target of the moment? I am not convinced that modern fly tying isn't presenting a whole series of death-mask flies to trout. A lot of observation and experimentation is in order here before we completely abandon flies that have served fishermen so well for centuries.

Every year or so now a new series of nymphs is presented to fishermen, and each is highly acclaimed because it appears to our eyes even more faithful to the naturals than the previous attempts. The last group of imitations I saw had the precise number of tails (or setae) the naturals have, and six perfectly formed legs with the correct number of joints in each leg. They were every bit as realistic as the figures in Mme. Tussaud's waxworks. And, like those famous statues, they were also as stiff as boards because their realism had been achieved by stiffening the appendages of the flies with lacquer.

Flies like these deserve to be carefully mounted and exhibited, but it would be almost sacrilegious to fish with them. It might also be a waste of time. A few years ago there were many nymphs made of molded plastic that looked as if they could crawl out of their flybox compartments, and yet they were indifferent fishtakers and have nearly disappeared from the market. The shortcoming was that they, and many of the newer patterns formed with lacquered feathers, were designed from models that were the preserved corpses of nymphs. Have you ever watched a living mayfly nymph or stonefly larva underwater? The gills appear enormous, are fluttering constantly, and are very often quite different in color from the body of the insect.

There's a lot of evidence that the motion of these gills and the scampering movement of the legs identify these nymphs as living food to the trout, and that the precise color and size, though important, are secondary. Any stiff, lacquered imitation loses this seductive quality of movement and much of the natural insect's translucence as well. I admire these new photographically realistic nymphs as art forms, but they leave me lukewarm as lures for trout.

Perhaps the most compelling case of all for the old wet fly is that it moved and breathed with every subtle change in current. Wet flies, as we have noted, were probably designed to imitate many life phases of many types of insects, yet they can perform splendidly as imitations of mayfly nymphs when specifically tied for this purpose. The wet versions of the Light Cahill and March Brown, for example, with their darker, striped topsides, can be deadly imitations when the corresponding nymphs are hatching out. The secret here is to tie the wings in low and on the sides, as you would with a strip-wing salmon fly, so that they hug the top half of the body. Their silhouette is then sleek and nymphlike, yet there's still an extra "aliveness" to the play in the wing fibers that the standard nymph-dressing can't equal.

I have a whole series of wet flies like these—different from the ones duplicating emerging or drowned flies—and I have more confidence in them than I have in the popular nymph-dressings of the same insects. I'll admit I haven't tested these against the standard nymphs, two on a leader, the way I have the wet Quill Gordon, so I can't quote any catch figures. However, everything I've learned about trout and trout-fly tying, as well as my results, convince me that I'm on to a more productive style of fly.

To increase the breathing, moving characteristics of these patterns, I pluck out a lot of body dubbing with a needle or substitute ostrich herl dyed to an exact color for the body material. This increases the fly's similarity to a living nymph with its fluttering gills, and I'm sure this adaptation will increase the effectiveness of most nymph patterns, too.

I came upon this trick, which is certainly not original, after many years of learning the hard way. I didn't jump to this conclusion easily after hearing all those stories about the chewed-up tattered fly outfishing all others, although it is now one of the few pieces of fishing folklore I firmly believe. No, I had to be taught this lesson, piece by piece, by a kindly but self-serving expert.

Early in my fly-fishing career and before I tied my own flies, I often fished with an elderly gentleman who appeared to be uncommonly generous. He would press on me all sorts of wet-fly and nymph patterns during a day's fishing, and since good flies cost the princely price of a quarter apiece in those days, I looked upon him as a walking gold mine. However, at the end of each day's efforts he questioned me about the performance of each of the donated flies, and graciously accepted the slightly used artificials back into his own box. With my usual hawkeyed hindsight, I'm now convinced that the old bandit wasn't the least bit interested in my researches; he knew exactly what he was doing. He was using me to "warm up" his flies for him, to get them into shaggy, fish-catching shape while he used the ones that were already in vintage condition. It turned out to be the classic case of one hand washing the other. My weekly allowance was minute and his fly supply was almost infinite.

Imitation of some sort or other is probably the key to success with today's hard-pounded trout. But what sort of imitation? You can imitate an insect's overall behavior pattern, for instance. You can also imitate the small motions of its gills, tails, legs, and antennae. Or you can imitate its color, shape, and appendages down to the minutest detail. I doubt, however, that any single nymph-dressing can excel at all three types of duplication. You have to compromise somewhere and with nymphs I prefer to skimp on exact anatomical details. I feel my more alive patterns perform at least as well as the more static, more photographic, dressings when matching a specific emerging nymph, and that when I use them for random prospecting they are far superior.

The wet flies I use to represent winged emergers, drowned adults, and egg-layers seem to be without any major shortcomings.

Wings and legs are responsive and mobile without sacrifice of true-to-life detail. I can't fault them in accuracy, theory, or performance.

I think the easiest and most convincing type of wet-fly fishing, if you want to take it up or try it again, can be experienced at the end of a summer evening. Until the light gets too dim to see your fly on the water, fish the dry-spinner imitation of the spent mayfly you've seen fall to the water, and fish it dead drift. Then, for the last fly of the day, tie on a standard wet fly of the same size and color. Go downstream a short distance to the head of the pool below where the current begins to lose its chop, and cast your fly straight across stream, letting it swim till it comes to a stop directly below you. Repeat at one-step intervals until the water gets too slow to pull your fly through the arc in a satisfactory manner.

Feel your way carefully downstream with your feet, but be sure to feel your line and rod with equal sensitivity. You should get some thumping strikes and—if you don't strike back too quickly as I usually do—some exciting fish. If you're like me, you'll probably find that the night is absolutely black before you decide it's time to stop.

Even the most fastidious fly fisher should feel happy after this type of angling, for he has been an exact imitationist the entire time. This is not chuck-and-chance-it with a nondescript. He has been presenting the closest possible imitation of the fly of the moment to the fish in exactly the same manner in which the naturals are coming to them. Most important of all, at a time of day when he is likely to be bone-tired, the angler has not had to strain his eyes, strike on hunches, or worry about whether or not his fly is still floating.

If this experiment in wet-fly fishing convinces you there's something here, perhaps you'll tie and try the wet fly on other occasions, too. Not as a mere blob of food, but as an imitation of a specific life stage of an identified insect. If you keep an open mind and compare results with fishing companions, I think you'll find the drill exciting and rewarding. You won't be exploring a new frontier, but you will be adding a third dimension to your dry-fly/nymph style of trout fishing, and, when you start observing flies and fly behavior for yourself without relying on some other man's word, you'll find a whole new and productive world of fishing.

Every year sunk-fly men seem to add more weight to their flies, leaders, or lines to make sure their nymphs bump along the very bottom of the stream. No doubt this has made fly fishing more effective—especially when the trout aren't feeding. But it has also made casting and fishing less pleasant. So much so that many anglers will spin or bait-fish rather than torture their rods and their arms in this manner.

The wet-fly fishing I'm practicing and proposing takes a middle ground and covers the middle depth of the water. Here you don't need sash-weights or heavy lead-core lines because emergers, egg-layers, and drowned flies don't hug the bottom the way nymphs do. They're not far under the surface, and you can present their counterfeits realistically with regular tackle and a floating line. Surprisingly often, this is exactly what the trout ordered.

It seems that fly fishing becomes more complicated and technical every year, and perhaps this is necessary to achieve best results under demanding circumstances. But shouldn't fly fishing be a joy as well as a challenge? Men in less harried times certainly thought so. They fished the wet fly with grace and pleasure, not feeling that every fish in the stream had to be yanked out of it. The surprising thought is that they just may have been using the most effective imitation of all.

1976

13

A Midsummer Night's Dream Fly

That sudden, midseason rise at dusk
is seldom caused by a hatch of duns.
It calls for a totally different tie.

Strange things happen on trout streams during warm, mid-summer evenings. Just before the bats fly, pools that have seemed lifeless all day suddenly dimple with rings of rising trout. This is exactly what the patient fly fisherman has hoped for, but he still faces a problem: He can't detect any flies on the water. What, then, have the trout started to feed on? And what do you match when there's no hatch?

This situation frustrated me for years. Whatever I floated over those dimpling fish—standard duns, caddisflies, big variants, or minute midges—usually drew only halfhearted false rises and, on some evenings, not even that. After waiting all day for that witching half hour, it was galling to draw a blank while trout sipped all around me.

I got my first clue to solving this puzzle by rereading Art Flick's
Streamside Guide. He recommended a sparsely tied Red Quill in #14
or #16 as a killing fly for late-evening fishing. Since Flick had a gift
for keeping things simple, he just might have considered this all-
purpose pattern a "near-enough" imitation of a dying, or spent-
wing, mayfly.

The following evening, I tried a standard #16 Red Quill over
several regular risers, but they would have none of it. Had the fish
become more selective and demanding since Flick's day? There

seemed only one way to find out whether or not spent-wing patterns were the answer. I pulled out a pair of scissors, snipped off the upright wings, then pruned the hackle, top and bottom, until the fly was shaped like an airplane. The result was not elegant, but at least I had a fly that would float flush in the surface film on what looked like outspread wings.

On the first cast, my fly disappeared even though I knew where it should have landed. Fearing that I'd overpruned the artificial and that it had sunk, I twitched my line. A small wake proved to me that my fly was, indeed, on the surface. It was just floating so flush in the surface film that I couldn't see it thirty-five feet away in the fading light. Any spent-winged natural, I reasoned, would also be invisible on the water.

I managed to take one good fish on that fly before I left it in the jaws of a deceptively large trout by striking too hard. By then, there wasn't enough light left to trim and tie on another, but I felt I was finally on the right track.

To back up my hunch that spent wings were the mystery flies, on my next outing I lugged along a yard of fine netting. I held this in the water at the tail of a pool for a minute or so just at quitting time and then ran back to my car to check my catch in the headlights. Sure enough, there were eight or ten small, glassy-winged mayflies lying spread-eagle in the meshes.

Where had all these spent wings come from? I had seen no flushes of hatching mayflies during the afternoon or early evening. But I had noticed the odd fly fluttering off the water all during the day. These occasional emergers were not concentrated enough to start trout rising. But apparently, they really added up because they hatched out over such a large area and long time period. When they fell to the water during a few minutes and funneled down a narrow feed lane, they created a sizable "hatch."

While a pruned-down, standard dry fly makes a passable imitation, it's a shame to deface choice, stiff-hackled flies. It's wiser to carry a few simple and more realistic patterns.

I tie these up with slightly overlength tails, split in two to form a "V." Bodies are made of quill or thin hackle stems to keep them slim. Wings are easy: I wind on several turns of longish, pale dun hackle, then trim off the top and bottom fibers. Even a beginner can turn out this rugged pattern and there's no need to use top-grade hackle. Good imitations of spent-wing mayflies—those with gauzy, translucent wings—are surprisingly hard to find in most tackle shops. If you don't tie yourself, have a tying friend or your local pro run some up for you.

I've found I need only two patterns. The most useful of these has pale dun wings and tails and a reddish-brown quill body; I use this in #16 some 90 percent of the time. However, if I've seen mostly pale yellow mayflies hatching out, I put on a yellow-bodied fly tied in the same manner. A few of each tied on #14, #16, and #18 hooks are all I've ever found necessary. In fact, I've never quite been able to convince myself I really need that second yellow imitation. I doubt that trout can detect much color in the dim evening light, and it's probably the silhouette of the fly against the darkening sky above that fools them.

And fool them it does. I can't think of another type of fly that is taken with such all-out confidence. False rises to this imitation are extremely rare, and most fish are hooked securely—some even well back in the throat. Since they see this style of dry fly so rarely, perhaps they don't associate it with the standard dun patterns that have pricked or hooked them earlier in the season.

Fishing these flies effectively is nearly as simple as tying them. You do have to present them drag-free, though, because dead flies don't twitch or flutter. A dead-drift float is usually no big problem because you'll be casting over flat, slow water that doesn't have the braids and current tongues that pockets, runs, or heads of pools usually do. Still, you can eliminate any hint of unnatural drift if you angle your cast nearly straight upstream to the fish.

To make the most of those last precious minutes of daylight, your actions must be disciplined and deliberate. You'll have time to take only two, perhaps three, trout, so you'll need to make every second count. But that doesn't mean you should rush.

Before the rise starts, reel in and examine your leader tippet. If it's too heavy or has picked up a knot, replace it with two feet of 2-

pound test. Tie on the small spent wing that should be your last fly of the day. Now, while there's still plenty of light and there are no rises to distract you, is the time to make sure your tackle is in perfect order.

Take a stand about three-quarters of the way down a long, slow pool where you have the best view of the pool's bottom half. This is where the most rising trout will show. As rise-forms start to appear, resist the temptation to step in and begin casting. Wait until the trout are feeding strongly and regularly.

You should put this waiting time to good use, though. These last few minutes are too valuable to squander on tiddlers, so pick out the two or three better-than-average trout that will become your targets.

This may sound hard to do when all the fish are dimpling like small dace, but there are telltale signs. The best trout will take over the choicest feeding positions and these will almost certainly be in the center thread of the slow current where the heaviest traffic of naturals is found. Concentrate your attention there.

Also keep in mind that big fish displace more water than small ones, no matter how gently they're sipping. When you see the water surface undulate slightly near the spreading rise ring, odds are you've spotted a sizable fish.

Once you've picked out your target fish, slide stealthily into position. Advancing waves on that glassy surface can quickly put down rising trout. Position yourself well below your first quarry—directly below if pool depth permits.

Present your fly only a foot or so above the rise-form so that only the finest strand of your leader falls on the fish's window. If you don't get a take on your first presentation, let your fly drift well below the lie before you pick it off the water—and do that as quietly as possible. Dry your fly with a couple of false casts, but make these off to one side so droplets of water won't spatter down near the fish. Now pitch the fly to the fish again and don't give up too soon. Your fly is competing with a lot of naturals. I've had fish take firmly and confidently on the twentieth cast.

Since you'll rarely see your fly, it's almost impossible to tell from a rise-form whether the trout has taken your artificial or a nearby natural. You will know, though, at least within a square foot or so, where the fly should be. Any ring appearing in that area should be treated as a take. But don't strike—at least not in the conventional manner. A sharp jerk of your rod will rip your fly across the surface, frightening a natural taker, or it could cause a breakoff in the event that a heavy fish has the fly in its mouth.

Just raise your rod tip slowly and firmly, feeling for the fish. Trout will hold spent wings in their mouths for several seconds before ejecting them. You have plenty of time to pull the fly steadily and firmly into the corner of the trout's jaw.

After you've taken the downstream fish, slide on up to the next good one you marked down. There's no need to change or even oil your spent wing. A couple of brisk false casts and it will again float flush in the surface tension.

Midsummer trouting has its own special rewards. You usually catch your biggest dry-fly fish of the year during July and August— even if you quit at dark. Prime taking time may be shorter than it is in May and June. But it is sweeter. Springtime fishing usually drops off toward twilight and you finally reel in after poorer and poorer results. Not so in summer. You'll usually catch your best fish of the day only seconds before you quit. And I can't think of a better ending to any day than that.

1989

PART 3

the tackle

14

How to *Buy* Superior Trout Flies

All flies—even those from the same tyer—
are not created equal. Here's how to pick out
the best from the bins.

That's right, I said "buy."

There are dozens—probably hundreds—of books in the fishing library that will tell you how to *tie* flies. But I've never seen even a magazine article that tells you how to *buy* them, have you?

This is an astonishing omission. Less than a quarter of the trout fishermen I know tie their own flies. The majority of us have to buy, borrow, or steal the flies we fish with and we need all the help we can get. But what should we look for—and look out for—to select the finest individual flies available?

The obvious first step is to find out which professional tyer tackle store in your area offers flies of the best design and highest quality feathers. This is the easy part. Just ask the most expert anglers or amateur fly tyers you know and they'll narrow your choice down to one or two shops.

Once you've located the best source, you're still not halfway home. This is because all flies—even those made by the same tyer—are definitely *not* created equal.

You need to know the subtler points of fly excellence to end up with the few superior examples from the dozen or two displayed in the showcase bin. And, since dry flies are the most demanding of all patterns, let's start in their bin.

Because floating flies have to be tied on relatively heavy hooks, all of them will try their darnedest to sink partially or completely. The feathers best equipped to exploit surface tension and resist sogginess are rooster hackles, and these necks vary widely in quality.

Top-notch, dry-fly hackle is stiff and springy. The best way to check for this is to rub the hackle collar across your lower lip. If you feel a prickly sensation, good. When, on the other hand, the fibers feel soft, like a camel's hair paintbrush, watch out. The best dry-fly hackle fights back.

A secondary test can be made by examining the fly against a strong light. If the hackle fibers glint and the tip ends appear translucent, this should reconfirm your original assessment. If, however, hackle spikes look dull, or even chalky, they're probably second-rate. Since most of the flies in the same bin have usually been tied with hackles from the same neck, when two or three samples of the same bin flunk both of the above tests, you should save your money and spend it elsewhere.

Once you're satisfied with hackle quality, you can focus your attention on proportion or design. Even though every fly in the entire showcase has probably, as we've said, been dressed by the identical tyer, no two specimens are exactly alike. The choicest floaters will be a little bit—sometimes even a lot—better than the poorest of the bunch.

The classic, mayfly dun imitation is the end-product of over a century of trial and error and is still the most popular style of floating fly. Both its wings and tail should be the same length as the straight part of the hook shank. The radius of its hackle collar should be one and a half times as long as the hook-gape or about three-quarters as long as the wings. Any fly that varies visibly from these proportions probably won't cock or float on the water properly and should be left in its bin for a customer who doesn't know, or care, as much as you do.

If you fish mainly fast-water, freestone streams, select the bushier dressings that will float higher and longer on choppy water. If, on the other hand, your home waters are mostly placid limestoners or spring creeks, you'll be better off with the sparser dressings. Slow-water trout have plenty of time to eyeball your artificial and, here, lighter hackled, more realistic flies will usually score better.

The tails on floaters #16 or larger should be substantial because these few fibers are called upon to do Herculean work. First, they must create enough wind-resistance, as the fly flutters down to the surface, so the fly will alight with the hook-shank horizontal, rather than bend-down. This is a demanding task, considering all that bushy hackle wound around the opposite end of the hook. Second, these tail fibers must get a strong enough grip on the surface tension to keep this heavier end of the hook from sinking during a long float. I know full well that mayflies have only either two or three tails (although I'm convinced that trout *don't*), but wimpy, skimpy tails just aren't up to the flotation task.

Due to the natural curve in the hackle fibers of many necks, some tails will flair quite widely. Everything else being equal, these are the ones that will flutter down, and float, best.

Wings deserve more than casual scrutiny. Whether they're made of hair, plumage, hackle tips, or slips of quill, they should be positioned dead center on top of the hook and each wing should be of the same size, length, and bushiness. They should be separated from each other by an angle of 25 to 45 degrees. Anything within that range is acceptable as long as both wings veer from the vertical at the same angle.

Wings made from slips of primary wing feathers call for an additional test. If they're not perfectly aligned along the longitudinal axis of the fly in exactly the same plane, they can twist a leader-tippet like the rubber band inside a model airplane. Hold the fly with the hook bend away from you and look it squarely in the eye. Reject any that aren't absolutely symmetrical.

Bodies are the least troublesome feature of a dry fly. Whether they're tied out of herl, quill, or fur-dubbing, check to be sure they're neat and gently tapered.

Caddisfly floaters aren't nearly as demanding, so I'll touch on only the most popular style of tie: the Elkhair Caddis. Make sure the fly you select out of the bin has a wing that envelopes at least the top 180 degrees of the hook shank. Flies with the hair clumped on top of the hook only don't ride as high and jauntily as those with wings that are furled around the hook shank and body.

There's one other type of floating fly you shouldn't be without and that's the versatile variant. Variants are simply wingless dry flies tied with oversized hackles on smallish hooks. Hackle radius should measure nearly three hook-gapes instead of the standard one and a half and, to balance out the fly, tails should be nearly twice the usual length.

Variants are exciter flies and the higher they sit above the surface, the more tempting they become. Because of this, hackle quality is even more important—if that's possible—than in conventional floaters. When, or if, you locate a batch with exceptional hackles—stock up. Buy up a supply that will last you for several years. Super variants are as scarce as roosters' teeth.

Fortunately, these are quite durable flies and you won't need a wide range of patterns. I've found the three recommended by Art Flick are quite sufficient. The ginger-and-grizzly Gray Fox is my all-time favorite and the Dun is nearly as good. I've had only so-so results with the Cream Variant during daylight hours, but, because you can see it at least fifteen minutes longer at dusk, it makes a great last-fly-of-the-day selection.

Wet flies have yielded a lot of ground—or should that be water?—to nymphs in recent years, but I'd feel deprived if I couldn't carry a few of the classic favorites. I'm especially devoted to the Light Cahill, Gold-ribbed Hare's Ear, Leadwing Coachman, and that oddball attractor, the Rio Grande King.

When selecting individual wet flies, give preference to those with small, neat heads. These give wets a clean entry and better swimming characteristics. Wings should be of equal size and length and should be positioned symmetrically. It's best if they lie low along the body, enveloping the top half of the body so they appear like tops of nymphs' bodies.

Let your choice err on the side of the sparser ties. Most wets have far too much wing and hackle. The tips of the hackle should not quite reach the point of the hook and, the fewer their number, the better the fly will keel. Don't make the mistake of feeling that you need bulky dressings to catch a trout's attention. They can see, and do feed on, minute organisms. *More* is seldom better. Give the trout as little as possible to find fault with.

I've never been able to figure out whether all-hackle flies were true wet flies or nymphs, so I'll treat them together. These are the least demanding style of flies. Again, tilt toward the sparser-hackled examples. After all, nymph naturals have only six legs.

The majority of nymphs come with spun-fur bodies and you should check for an even, insect-body taper. Again, I prefer the slim, suggestive ties over the bulky ones and I like to pick out some fur fibers to make them appear more translucent.

Last, but not least, we come to streamers and bucktails. In one sense, these are just wet flies with extra-long wings. So inspect an individual fly the way you would a wet . . . look them in the eye and be sure that wings and hackle are symmetrical. If a streamer fly is tied off-kilter, it will wobble when retrieved through the water and this, somehow, subtracts from its fish-appeal.

In another sense, though, streamers are quite different. They are tied to represent small minnows rather than insects. Since most trout patterns run from an inch and a half to three inches long, they're imitations of baitfish that are either small, young, or both. Most of these bite-sized minnows are quite translucent—young smelt especially—so the best representations are sparsely tied out of semitransparent materials.

Wings made out of whole hackle feathers are sinuous, let some light pass through them, and are an excellent choice. Wings tied out of bucktail, on the other hand, tend to be opaque and too stiff for smallfish flies. Polar bear hair is beautifully translucent when wet, but it, too, is a bit stiff in shorter lengths. My favorite "bucktail" hair is calf tail, naturally white or dyed—especially if taken from tails that are straight-haired and glossy. Trout streamers should undulate. The popular marabous are tops at this. I only wish their fibers weren't so solid-looking and opaque.

Wherever trouters get together, you hear a lot of chatter about the latest fly-rod tapers and the smoother drags on new reels. But I hear little serious debate about flies, such as are parachute ties better than thorax flies or are the classic dressings still the best. I can't understand this. Trout aren't attracted or deceived by rods, reels, lines, or leaders.

The first and great commandment of fly fishing is so simple and self-evident that it is often forgotten. *The only part of your tackle any fish should ever see is your fly.*

So it has to follow that the surest way to increase your catch— or catch-and-release—is to offer the trout the very finest flies you can buy.

1994

15

A Gut Reaction

Synthetics may be cheaper and
maintenance-free, but the old silkworm
gut leaders were, in some ways, superior.

Unless you're currently receiving Social Security payments or are approaching eligibility, chances are slim that you've ever fished with a silkworm gut leader. And that's a pity because gut was a joy to fish with despite its few drawbacks.

One inconvenience was that gut had to be stored between wet felt pads to keep it pliable and reliable or, if carried dry, it had to be soaked for fifteen to twenty minutes before it could be used safely. This may seem unbearable to today's hurry-up generation, but these waiting minutes, when used to identify hatching insects, mark down rising fish, and plot your place of entry into a pool could actually increase the angler's chances of success.

Then, too, gut demanded regular attention. Finer tippets began to fray after several hours of constant casting and had to be checked periodically for weakness. Again, this may not have been as onerous as it sounds because, unless you're a Joan Wulff, you should probably check your tippet for wind knots from time to time, anyway.

One solid complaint against gut accuses it of having been expensive and to this I have no rebuttal. A good leader or a dozen tippets would cost well over $5 today in inflation-adjusted dollars. Such a price, I'll admit, could dampen the rising popularity of fly fishing and leave it open to the old indictment of elitism.

A final disadvantage of gut was that it tested far weaker than modern materials. To this I have to answer "Yes, but . . . " and that "but" is a very big one. Certainly synthetic monofilaments are rated as twice as strong as gut of the same diameter, but the testing methods give misleading results.

Laboratory tests on leader materials are conducted under "slow load" conditions. This means that the poundage of pull is increased gradually until breakage occurs and the final reading before the snap is recorded as the strength of that particular fiber.

But this isn't how most leaders are broken while fishing. Some 95 percent of all failures occur during the strike, which is a "fast load" situation. And this is where gut excelled. It was actually stronger than listed when subjected to sudden stress, while modern monos are far weaker than rated when pulled quickly. A 6X gut tippet was remarkably tolerant of a hamfisted strike, while synthetics tend to pop at the knot when treated this way.

Gut also had many other characteristics that would endear it to today's anglers. First of all, it required only the simplest of knots

and these held with bedrock reliability. A simple Turle (no need for a double one or the improved clinch), which presented the fly in a straight line as though an extension of the leader, was guaranteed not to slip—ever. It was all you needed to kill the largest salmon and the longer you played a fish the tighter the knot became. I never heard of a gut-tied Turle slipping, and this knot is blessedly easy to tie even with frozen fingers.

Gut not only gave you the benefit of the doubt when you struck a fish too hard, but it was also forgiving of other sins. Being stiffer than nylon, gut tippets collected fewer of those mysterious wind knots.

And, even when one appeared out of nowhere, it weakened the tippet only slightly, not catastrophically, as is the case with most synthetics. I once killed a 20-pound Atlantic Salmon on 1X gut only to discover, to my horror, that there had been, not one, but three wind knots in the tippet during the long struggle. With nylon, it would have been just another story of the big one that got away.

In presenting a fly, whether wet or dry, gut offered two further advantages. One was that it absorbed water regularly and tended to sink. This meant that small wets and nymphs stayed submerged and didn't skirt along the surface. And, especially on sunny days, it was comforting to know that the tippet near your dry fly was well sunk and not in the surface film casting a cablelike shadow on the stream bottom.

Curve casts were far easier to execute with the stiffer gut leader. The dump or "S" casts are now more widely used to prevent drag because of the limpness of nylon, but I feel they don't let you place your fly as accurately as the old curve did.

Lastly, the stiffness of gut made dropper flies stand away from the leader, seldom winding themselves around it in a useless, clinging spiral. I can't help but believe that the useful and killing sunk dropper fly has all but dropped out of sight simply because modern monofilaments can't present it properly.

So, there you have it. Gut, for all its faults, could do a lot of things modern materials can't. And I can promise you that fly fishers did—and still can—catch at least as many trout with yesteryear's terminal tackle as they do with today's highly touted synthetics.

1992

16

The Ultimate Fly Rod

Fiberglass and graphite may be
lighter and stronger, but there's
something sublime about split-cane.

Men are emotional about fly rods. Trout rods in particular, yet perhaps even about the hefty rods used in salt water for bonefish and tarpon, or about freshwater rods used for bass bugging and streamer fishing. Men may love a salmon rod. But light, split-cane fly rods are objects of reverence. A Payne, Halstead, Gillum, Garrison, Leonard, Orvis, Winston, Young, Thomas, or an Edwards trout rod may well be the most cherished piece of equipment used in any sport.

The only serious rival is the wing-shooter's fine double shotgun. In fact, fly rod and shotgun have much in common. Both are used in the beauty of the wild outdoors. And both become intimate extensions of the body in motion. In some respects, though, the fly rod is the more intimate companion. It seems to be alive. It bends and moves in response to the angler's touch. The rod is a more constant friend, too. Fishing seasons are longer than shooting seasons, and, while a bird shooter may fire several times in a day afield, the trouter will number his casts in the thousands.

Add to this that a day on his favorite stream is a semireligious experience for the dedicated angler. The trout stream is set apart from other scenes of sport—by hemlock and rhododendron, willow, and warbler, the play of sunlight on a riffle. Many fine authors have tried to capture this magic, but it begs description. A great naturalist once described a stream as "the artery of the forest." It is that and more. It is also the life blood of the trouter.

In this setting and in this spirit, a rod becomes far more than just a tool for casting. And, fortunately, this bond between rod and man is an especially happy one. The experienced angler seldom blames his rod. In fact, he is all too liable to consider it perfection.

This happiness with things as they are can be observed in almost any fine tackle store. There are seldom requests for unconventional rod actions or special embellishments. If you examine a sampling of rods by the finest makers, you will see that they are almost uniformly modest in appearance. The brown cane glows warmly through the clear varnish. The reel seat is a harmonious cedar or walnut. Windings will usually be a neutral tan. This is the quiet beauty of the partridge, not the gaudy beauty of the cock pheasant.

And yet, despite the generic description above, each maker subtly signs his own work. Custom-made reel fittings differ from one another. The shape of the cork grip often indicates the maker. And then there's the cane itself. Most Leonards are quite light-colored. So are Garrisons and Gillums. Paynes are medium brown. Halsteads and Orvises are quite dark brown.

Any of these fine rods is fairly expensive. One may cost from $150 to perhaps slightly more than $250 (circa 1969). But it is definitely not a rich man's plaything, or a status symbol. A great many of these rods are in the hands of people of very modest means. I once saw a farmer fishing with a Gillum in the stream that ran behind his barn. When I admired the rod he looked a bit sheepish and admitted, "I've always wanted one of these, and then I made a bit of extra money trapping last winter. But my wife sure doesn't know how much I paid for it." You can be sure that many lunches have been skimped or skipped in order to pay for a dream rod.

Is a $250 bamboo rod ten times as good as a $25 glass rod? There's no pat answer. It all depends on your sense of values.

Everett Garrison, one of the very finest custom makers, can back up his art with some science. "A glass rod doesn't throw the smooth curve of line that a fine bamboo does. Stop-motion photography proves this." All well and good, but why do most tournament distance casters now use glass? "It's a very powerful material, all right," Garrison admits. "But they haven't got the tapers worked out yet. Perhaps some day."

There's more to it than that. There's a "sweet feel" to a great bamboo rod that just can't be duplicated. When you're casting thousands of times a day, this advantage may be worth a lot in pure enjoyment—even if it won't catch more fish. A bamboo rod should last the average fisherman at least twenty years. That comes to $12.50 per year, or merely the price of two tankfuls of gas. When you look at it that way, a great rod isn't an extravagance.

There's a joker in that twenty-year life expectancy, though. It's only a median figure. A rod may last a man a lifetime if he fishes only several times a year. On the other hand, the screen door has ended the life of many a rod before it delivered its first cast. Each year hundreds of fine rods are crushed underfoot, splintered against tree trunks, or chopped off by car doors. Surprisingly, rod breakage while actually playing a trout is one of the rarest forms of disaster.

Perhaps it isn't fair to measure a rod's life in terms of years. Barring accidents, it should be measured in numbers of casts. For each time a bamboo rod flexes, it dies a little. It may take years to notice a change in power and action, for an angler unwittingly suits his casting style to the rod in hand. But fatigue is inexorable. The finest, steeliest dry-fly rod I ever owned—or ever handled for that matter—was an eight-foot Halstead. I still own it and cherish it, but I seldom fish with it. After some seven hundred and fifty days of dogged dry-fly fishing, it's a slow, lazy parody of its former self.

All great rods don't die; some escape both catastrophe and senility. But they survive in collections, like pinned insects, as a matter of record. In one notable collection is a priceless "gold" rod. Its history belongs to a brasher era, when the president of a kerosene company (which grew into Standard Oil) refused to be outdone by royalty. When this captain of industry heard that Queen Victoria had a rod with all-gold fittings, he decided to match her. He commissioned America's top rodmaker to make him a rod with all-gold ferrules and reel seat—then had all the metal intricately engraved by the finest gun engraver of the day!

In the same collection is a more modest, yet more historic rod. It was the favorite of Theodore Gordon, who, before his death in 1915, pioneered and established dry-fly fishing in America. The many excellent rods of the great Edward R. Hewitt seem to have escaped the collectors, even though Hewitt died only about a dozen years ago. His grandchildren don't know where they all went. Have they fallen unceremoniously into the hands of the great-grandchildren? I hate to think that these rods might be suffering the same fate as my grandfather's ten-foot Thomas. I well remember using it with a quarter-ounce sinker, fishing for flounders off Cape Ann, Massachusetts, when I was a larcenous and untutored eight-year-old.

Sadly, great rods are being ruined or retired faster than they are being built. Demand for the very finest easily exceeds supply in our affluent society.

One hundred years ago, production was also negligible. The ardent angler made his own rods and perhaps a few extras for his friends; these rods of ash, lancewood, or greenheart, while finely finished and ferruled, were relatively simple in construction. Rod guides were often simple unbraced rings which flopped as the line struggled through. Samuel Phillippe changed all this.

The art of lamination had been used in older bows; in the early nineteenth century, English rod tips of three-part design were used, and some glued work must have appeared then. Phillippe was an Easton, Pennsylvania, gunsmith who fished. He made violins as well. With the skill of a minor Stradivarius, he revolutionized the trout rod.

What was probably the first entire split-cane rod appeared in America in 1848—Phillippe's "rent and glued-up cane" rod, as it was called then. He wisely chose the six-part, hexagonal cross-section, which offers a flat, glued plane for flexion. Nine-, eight-, five-, and four-segment rods would be tried and discarded.

Phillippe's son, Solon, and later Charles Murphy, learned from the master. In 1870, the great self-taught builder Hiram L. Leonard began varnishing wonderful rods in Bangor, Maine. Thomas, Edwards, and the elder Edward Payne, whose son James became the finest rodbuilder who ever touched a plane, learned at Leonard's bench.

George Parker Holden, a hobbyist and writer on rods many years ago, made his own, and trained Everett Garrison, an architect, who still builds by fits and starts for the custom trade. But Nat Uslan, who learned from Payne, has retired. Edwards has died, and so has Thomas, though his company is still in business, making fine rods.

Shortly before this article was begun, Jim Payne told a friend, "I'm leaving the shop, I don't know when I'll be back." He died one month later. The announcement of his death in the New York papers precipitated a run on Abercrombie & Fitch's stock of used Payne rods—his output had been low for years. Paynes have doubled in price; the big salmon rods, which he stopped making fifteen years ago, are worth $750, prime condition, against $150. Younger hands struggle to keep the Payne shop going. Pinkey Gillum, Payne's fine apprentice, who built rods independently for years, died eight years ago. The masters are not being replaced.

The Charles Orvis Company in Manchester, Vermont, must be credited with offering the contemporary angler a fine rod on the retail rack. Their twenty-five hundred pieces a year, along with the production of Young of Detroit, Winston of San Francisco, and Leonard of Rockland County, New York, barely touch present demand, despite the inroads of glass. Very little that is wonderful is coming out of England or France, and the Japanese seem to have failed as rodmakers.

What makes one rod great, another mediocre? Materials and workmanship. The trout rod is pared to an irreducible minimum, a trend that began when the dry-fly method reached fad proportions under Theodore Gordon's tutelage in the early 1900s. False casting, short float, and recasting made the old ten-foot rods instruments of torture after an hour or so of fishing. Builders competed for lightness by sixteenths of an ounce. While the salmon rod remained a symphony, the dry-fly rod became a quartet. The slightest flaw in taper or action is quickly transmitted to the hand. The real devotee pursues his jewel-sided quarry with bamboo; glass is rare in the top trout clubs.

Bamboo, the muscle and sinew of the rod, is a large grass of which there are many species, sizes, and qualities. The first rods—perhaps Phillippe's original rods—were built of Calcutta bamboo. Today this is porch furniture bamboo, not rod material.

Modern rods are built of what is called Tonkin bamboo, said to be found only in a small area in southern China. One legend has it that only those stalks that grow in the hilltops are first rate, because they have been strengthened by resisting the wind. Another story is that this bamboo has ceased to exist in a wild state and is a cultivated crop. Most likely, there are several species of bamboo that have the desired strength and straightness for rod building.

A store of well-aged and dried canes of this type is the rod-maker's bank account. They are eight feet long, three inches in diameter, and may have cost only $2 apiece. They are the first key to quality, as is the stock of hackle necks or a particular strain of live roosters to a fly tyer.

But even a plentiful supply of the best cane is no assurance of perfect materials, for individual canes must be specifically selected for special tasks. Here a knowledge of the microscopic construction of bamboo and how it works is essential. A cross-section of a piece of bamboo reveals small, powerful fibers that run the length of the section of cane and are embedded in a relatively neutral, but binding, matrix. A closer examination of this cross-section reveals that these fibers are very close together on the outside of the cane, or nearest the exterior enamel, and that they become less and less dense as you approach the pithier interior.

A rodmaker examines this cross-section very carefully as he selects a cane for a particular purpose. If he is going to build a seven-and-a-half-foot dry-fly rod, he looks for a cane with a dense cluster of fibers on the outside edge. He may have to examine and discard several canes to find this type. On the other hand, he may find one with an exceptionally dense power structure running well into the interior. This is a special prize, but not for the seven-and-a-half-foot trout rod. All of those prized and rare inner power fibers would be planed away in making a rod of narrow diameter. This cane he marks and puts away as a special cane for use in a larger, more powerful salmon rod.

Only when a suitable cane has been selected from an already highly selected batch of bamboo can the work properly commence. This consists of turning a single piece of cane into a fly rod of several sections, each of which is made up of six separate but absolutely equal slices of bamboo. While this fact of hexagonal structure is widely known, it is also often the sum total of an angler's knowledge about bamboo rods—even among men who own several of the finest. Yet this is about the same as a sports car driver knowing only that all cars have four wheels!

Actually, the hand making of a fine rod is part art, part craftsmanship, and it is a lengthy and painstaking process. Here are some of the major steps involved in the order that some, but not all, rodmakers follow.

First, the selected cane is split in half and the partitions inside each node are cut out with a gouge. If the rod is to be the popular seven-and-a-half-footer, in two pieces and with an extra tip, one half is split into six equal sections and put aside for the butt section. The other half is split into twelve pieces for the two tips. The pieces forming each section are cut and arranged with the nodes staggered so that no two fall opposite each other. Pieces are numbered so they can be reassembled in the same sequence.

Each piece is then placed in a V form, and the two split sides planed to an angle. The nodes, which protrude slightly on the enamel side, are then filed approximately flush, and now the eighteen strips are ready for straightening. If the bamboo had been sawed into strips—as is the case with many high-quality rods made by larger concerns—this step would not be necessary. But Tonkin cane grows straight once in a blue moon; normally, split-cane sections veer off a few degrees at each node, and it is at these awkward natural joints that the rodmaker sets to work.

Fortunately, bamboo has very plastic qualities when heated to a certain, rather high temperature. By holding the node over a small lamp and turning it carefully to prevent burning or charring, bamboo may be straightened by applying moderate pressure, and the strip will hold its shape after it has cooled.

The straightened strips are then heat-treated to give them the extra steely quality that even well-seasoned cane does not possess. It would be easier to do this baking after they had been planed to size, but the process causes some shrinkage that might make the final rod thinner than planned. It is best to heat-treat before planing even though the extra hardness will make the planing a bit more difficult.

Hours of this delicate work make all six pieces of each section alike to within one-thousandth of an inch. The strip is placed into a V form which has caliper adjustments every several inches; all six pieces comprising that section are cut flush to the form. Only two sides of the strip may be worked on. A cut off one side. Turn the strip. A cut off the other. Near the end of this process, the enamel, which has no power, is removed with one clean stroke. No further planing on the rind side is permissible on a fine rod.

From the artisan's point of view, the rod is now done; its final action and feel have been fully imprinted into the bamboo. Of course, there are many hours of work left: gluing and pressure-winding the strips, trueing them up, seating the ferrules, fitting the grip and reel seat, winding and fixing the guides, and three coats of varnish. But though it must be meticulously done, all this is journeyman's work.

A top rodmaker says it takes him a minimum of twenty-five hours to make a rod. Working hours—not counting the hours and days he must wait for glue or varnish to set. I think he's underestimating his labor considerably.

When you consider that the top custom-made trout rods sold for as little as $100 only ten years ago, the economics of fine rod-making seems incredible. Without figuring in the rent, the materials, or the tools, the finest craftsmen in the field were probably making less than $4 an hour!

But these are proud and devoted men. You stand in line for a rod. Often you have to wheedle and cajole. I know one board chairman of a huge company who waited a year and a half for his nine-foot salmon rod. Finally he called the rodmaker and approached the matter with tact. He was told, "I haven't had time to start it yet. I'll call you when it's ready."

Another builder, troubled by telephone interruptions, calmly ripped the old-fashioned receiver off the wall and went on about his business.

It was a fine, monastic life, at $4 an hour.

The trade cannot possibly survive; the rods, and the tradition, do.

1969

17

Long Live the Long Rod

Is the short fly rod really less
fatiguing and more sporting?
Don't believe a word of it.

The most overrated piece of fishing equipment in America today
is the short fly rod. It is the least effective, least comfortable, and
least sporting angling tool ever invented. I know it's risky to knock
another man's woman, dog, or favorite rod, but a close look at the
evidence will only confirm my position.

At first glance it may seem that the choice between a short or
a long rod for stream fishing is simply a matter of whim. After all,
a fairly skilled caster can lay out sixty or seventy feet of line with a
tiny rod—more than enough distance for most trout-stream situations. But, keeping out of sight of the fish is only a small part of
the game. What is important is the ability to present the right fly
in a way that deceives the trout, and then to hook those you've
fooled. This is what separates the anglers from the casters. And it
is exactly here that the stubby rod shortchanges you.

A short rod leaves far too much line on the water while you're
fishing out the average cast. Every extra foot of this is a crippling

disadvantage, whether you're presenting a dry fly, wet fly, nymph, streamer, or (forgive me, Federation of Fly Fishers) live bait.

Suppose, for example, you're casting to a fish thirty feet away. With a six-foot rod, tip held high, you'll probably still leave eighteen feet of line and leader on the water when you make your presentation. (A bit more when fishing upstream, a bit less when working downstream.) On the other hand, with a ten-foot rod, casting under the same conditions, only about ten feet of terminal tackle—perhaps just your leader—would be lying on the surface. Judge for yourself which presentation is most likely to give you a badly dragging dry fly or an underwater fly that's moving unnaturally and out of control.

Admittedly, the amount of line on the water isn't a critical factor when you're fishing a stillwater pond or lake. But on streams with braiding currents, tongues of fast water, and unpredictable eddies, the more line you have on the water the more likelihood of an unappetizing presentation of your fly.

It is also much easier to hook a fish when most of your line is off the water. You're in more intimate touch with your fly and you don't have to guess at how hard to tug to straighten out the esses in your line, overcome the friction of water, and finally set the hook. Over 90 percent of the trout broken off are lost at the strike. Examine the circumstances the next time you leave your fly in a fish; the problem usually is too much line on the water when the take occurs.

It took me years to learn these simple fly-fishing facts of life. The truth started to sink in only about a dozen years ago when I was fishing in the mountains of southern France. I was using a snappy, eight-foot rod (certainly a sensible length by eastern U.S. standards), but I wasn't catching many fish and almost no really good ones. This was slow, clear limestone water heavily fished by vacationers and constantly harvested by a troup of professional fishermen who supplied the local hotels. Any fish that had run this gauntlet and grown to decent size was as thoroughly trained as an astronaut.

The professionals finally showed me their secret—which they regarded more as common sense than as an ingenious technique.

They'd learned that, in this clear, slick water, they couldn't approach these fish from upstream. Neither could they give the trout a look at their leader. So they cast upstream to a rising or observed fish, but with a variation of the conventional method. They'd drop their fly— usually a sparsely dressed wet pattern on a light hook—just downstream of the trout's tail so the leader wouldn't pass over his head. When the tiny ripples from the fly's entry passed over the trout's nose, he would usually turn around to see what sort of insect had fallen into the water behind him. If the stunt was pulled of perfectly, all the trout could see now was the artificial sinking slowly downcurrent.

Any line splash or drag meant instant failure, and I began to see why these experts used long rods—ten to ten-and-a-half feet long, in fact. "With a rod of three meters (nine feet, ten inches) you are just beginning to fish." they told me.

I finally learned how to execute this presentation with occasional success after days of practice. But my eight-foot rod, even though it could throw seventy to eighty feet of line with ease, was a big handicap.

Fishermen I saw in the Pyrenees on the Spanish border had taken this theory one step further. They used rods twelve to fourteen feet long on those tumbling mountain streams and these kept so much line off the water there wasn't even a word for "drag" in their local patois. They would simply swing their fly (or more often maggot) directly upcurrent and let it drift back naturally, keeping in touch by raising the rod tip. They neither added nor took in line. And they took in trout with unbelievable regularity.

The implications of all this to the dry-fly man, with his almost paranoid fear of drag, are enormous. The perfect presentation of his fly has to be one dapped on the surface with no leader at all touching the water. This is true whether the offering is to be made dead-drift with the natural flow of the current or simply bounced on the surface like an egg-laying insect.

I proved this to my satisfaction several years ago after a neighbor had been given an ancient and enormous English fly rod. This awesome wand was a full twenty feet long, made of a solid wood called greenheart, and must have weighed over three pounds. However, it had a light, flexible tip, having been built when single strands of horsehair were used as leader tippets.

I found some pretext to borrow this rod for a couple of hours and, after I'd rigged it with a light line and fine leader, I headed for a nearby river. Once I got the hang of it, I could dap a fly on the surface thirty to thirty-five feet away and make it dance and hop there with no leader at all touching the water. Smart, overfished trout nearly herniated themselves to grab my fly. If I'd continued to use that rod the State Conservation Department would have named me Public Enemy No. 1. However, my friend soon retired that rod to his collector's case, and perhaps that was just as well. After two hours with that wagon tongue, I felt as if I'd slipped every disk in my back.

Going to the opposite extreme, you can cast and catch fish with no rod at all. This would give you a rod some twenty feet shorter than the old English muscle-builder I just described. Of course this would have to be the worst possible tackle for trouting, but not because you couldn't cover the water or land the fish.

The late Ellis Newman could take the reel off the rod and with his bare hand work out all ninety feet of a double-taper and keep it in the air, false casting.

Similarly, Lee Wulff once hand cast to a nearby salmon and played that full-grown fish to the beach with just the reel in his hand. No rod at all. Again, you might do that, too, with practice. You might even be able to dine out on this feat for weeks if you could tell the epic story with enough suspense and gusto. But I don't think you'd want to make a habit of fishing like that.

So you see, a fly rod isn't a necessity. It's merely a convenience and a comfort.

How can I say "comfort" after that twenty-footer nearly put me in bed under traction? And doesn't a long rod have to punish the angler more than a short one? Well, yes and no.

In the first place, sheer lightness in a rod doesn't necessarily mean less effort. The difference between a 2-ounce rod and a longer 5-ounce model, compared to the angler's total weight on the scales, is negligible. So rest assured that the longer, slightly heavier rod won't weigh you down.

I have fished with many superb casters who said they reveled in the lightness of their short rods. But how they huffed and puffed and sweated. They were using both arms, both shoulders, and their back to make those long casts with toy tackle. Double-hauling may be the ultimate technique for tournament casting, but it's about as placid a way to enjoy a summer evening as alligator wrestling.

The point is, ask not what you can do for the rod, but rather what the rod can do for you. With a long rod, a small movement of the arm or wrist will take any reasonable length of line off the water for the backcast because there really isn't that much line clutched by surface tension. The line then goes back over your head, straightens out and bends the rod backward. Now a minimal effort forward with forearm, wrist, or both and rod snaps back, propelling the line forward again. What could be easier than that? The rod has done most of the work for you. Your hand has moved a foot or so with very little exertion instead of moving three feet or so and bringing shoulder and back muscles into play, as well.

My experiences in France were not the only reason why my rods became longer about a dozen years ago. At approximately that time, I read an article in an outdoor magazine extolling the joys of mini-rod fishing. The author honestly admitted that he did, at first, have trouble avoiding drag with his shorter rod, but that he had solved this problem by holding the rod high above his head as he fished out every cast. Thus this six-footer, he claimed, was every bit as effective as an eight or eight-and-a-half-footer and (get this), because his rod weighed only 1³⁄₄ ounces, it was far less fatiguing to fish with. Anyone who subscribes to that theory should now hold his right arm fully extended over his head for two or three minutes and tell me how it feels. I can't recall seeing any more articles from this man and I can only assume that acute bursitis has prevented him from taking even a pencil in hand.

If a twenty-footer can break your back and a six-footer gives you too much drag and too much work, what should be the length of an efficient and comfortable fly rod? A lot depends on your physical makeup and your style of fishing. If you're a continuous and compulsive false caster who likes to fish pocket water upstream, where the effective float is a foot or less, any rod over eight feet might put your arm in a sling. If, on the other hand, your style is more deliberate and you spend most of your time on slower water where you may make less than ten casts per minute instead of nearly one hundred, you could probably handle a ten-footer with ease for a whole day's fishing.

And don't be misled by the "bushrod" addicts. They argue that you get hung up too often fishing small, overgrown streams if you use anything longer than a five-footer. But the fact is, you'll get hung up a lot with a very short rod, too, because any form of true casting here will put your fly and leader in the branches. A long-line presentation is seldom an effective way to fish a string of small potholes, anyway. Drag is instantaneous and disastrous with a lot of line out on this type of water. Here, you're far better off with the long rod, flipping or swinging your fly to the chosen spot while you make the extra effort to conceal yourself.

Use as long a rod as you comfortably can. I have been fishing for the past several years with an eight-and-a-half-foot bamboo that weighs 4½ ounces. I am now going through a trial marriage with a 9½-foot glass rod that weighs about the same. This liaison has been so enjoyable that I'm now searching for a ten-footer with the same qualities.

On salmon rivers where I make only four or five casts per minute, my favorite wet-fly rod is a ten-and-a-half-footer that works beautifully with a medium weight #6 line. But I'll admit that I have to drop back to an eight-and-a-half-foot stick for dry-fly fishing. I just can't false cast that often with the long rod—although that ten-and-a-half-footer is the most effortless wet-fly rod I've ever hefted. And let me repeat: I find all these rods, both trout and salmon models, comfortable for a full day's fishing.

In case you're interested, the man who wields these monster rods bears no resemblance to King Kong. I don't tip the scales at 140 pounds with chest waders, spare reels, and enough assorted fly boxes to drown me if I fall into deep water.

I'll have to admit, though, there's one disadvantage to long fly rods—and it's a beauty. When you've finally hooked a fish, the long

rod makes the fish grow stronger. That extra length gives the fish greater leverage against your hand.

Isn't this precisely what the short-rod people are espousing? That fish are now smaller and tamer so we must use tackle that magnifies the quarry? But aren't they actually doing just the opposite?

There are only two basic ways to measure a rod's ability to glorify the struggles of a fish. One is the weight or force it takes to bend the rod properly. This factor is usually printed on the rod, just in front of the cork grip, in terms of the weight of line it takes to bring out its action. I've seen a lot of six-foot rods that call for a #6 or #7 line to make them work properly. This means that it takes between 160 and 185 grains (437½ grains equal one ounce) of moving line to flex the rod adequately. My nine-and-a-half-footer, on the other hand, needs only a #4, or 120 grains to flex it to its optimum.

But there's still another factor that makes one rod more sporting than another for playing a fish. That's the leverage against your hand. With a fly rod—which must be considered a simple lever once a fish is hooked—the fulcrum is where the hand holds the rod. You don't need an M.I.T. degree to see that the mechanical advantage is approximately 66.66+ percent greater in favor of the fish and against the sportsman with a ten-foot rod than it is with a six-footer.

Despite this elementary fact, I am often accused of derricking small fish out of the water with a whacking great salmon rod. Fault my reasoning if you can: I'm convinced the shoe is on the other foot. I maintain that short-rodders are not only selling themselves short on presentation and overexercising themselves needlessly, but grinding down small fish with mechanically superior weapons, as well.

If you have followed my argument carefully so far and, hopefully, found it airtight, you're probably asking, "How can so many of nature's noblemen have been taken in by this cruel hoax?"

In the beginning, all rods were long. They were used to swing some lure out to the unsuspecting fish and to haul the catch back to shore again. They were very much like our present-day cane poles and probably just about as long.

Rods were still very long in the seventeenth century. Izaac Walton recommended a snappy, eighteen-foot, two-handed model as the best choice in his day. He and Charles Cotton dapped, dibbled, and dangled their flies (and worms and maggots) on the water with these mightly poles with killing effect on the trout.

In the following century the scientific progress of the industrial revolution reached the angling world. Fishing reels appeared on the market and soon became popular because they allowed fishermen to lengthen or shorten line easily and to play larger fish more effectively. But the rods themselves remained long.

One hundred years after that, in the not-too-distant 1800s, rods still averaged a sensible twelve feet. When dressed-silk fly lines and split bamboo were introduced, just after the midpoint of the century, rods grew shorter and lighter. After all, why should the angler stand there waving half a tree over the water when he could cast to the far bank and beyond with a zippy little ten-footer?

But along with these advances came another type of progress: overpopulation, overfishing, and pollution. Trout became fewer. Fishing no longer was the simple culling of nature's bounty as it had been in Walton's day. It needed a mystique, a philosophy, a reason-for-being. This Frederick M. Halford and other British Victorians readily provided, and their code soon spread across the Atlantic in a slightly modified form. If the sheer joy of catching fish was not a sure thing, at least there was the joy of casting. A day astream . . . the play of the sweet bamboo . . . the lovely hiss of the line . . . the fly cocked perkily on the sparkling riffle . . . who cares for a full creel with all this?

All the while, of course, anglers still secretly wanted to catch fish—and I suppose you do, too. But our artificial Victorian code insists that this be done only by improving our casting or presentation, or by tinkering up a bit better imitation of, say, the female Iron Blue Dun. Reverting to aboriginal tackle and the more varied presentations it puts at your fingertips has been unthinkable.

Well, I think it *is* thinkable. And, if you really want to catch more trout and enjoy more sport doing it, perhaps you should think about it, too. Going back to eighteen-foot poles might be a bit too much. But do try a new nine- or ten-footer. If a ribbon clerk like me can swing one all day long, you may be able to handle one like a conductor's baton.

Can't I, after all this, find at least one kind thing to say about our new short fly rods? Well, yes. Perhaps this:

I am reminded of the country sage's defense of bad breath. "It's mighty unpleasant, but it sure beats no breath at all." Same goes for short fly rods. They beat handlines, or no rods at all.

1974

PART 4
the tactics

18

Cashing in on Caddis

*Just switching to a sunk or floating
imitation isn't enough when the fish
are feeding on caddisflies.*

Younger fly fishers may find this hard to believe, but, only twenty-five years ago, caddisflies were considered a nuisance and crossed off as a "brush-hatch" that never reached the water. The average fly shop didn't carry any caddis imitations, either. Back then, I remember asking the late Art Flick why he barely mentioned caddis in his classic streamside guide. He thought for a moment and said, "I guess that's because, over on the Schoharie, where I do most of my fishing, we don't have much of a caddis problem."

Problem? With the exception, perhaps, of rich limestoners and spring creeks, caddis make up about half of the insect-food in running-water trout fisheries. That's certainly true of pool-and-riffle freestoners and because of the enormous build-up of plankton in stillwater impoundments, net-spinning caddis are actually the main course on our increasing number of tailwater fisheries.

The chief reason why caddis were once considered frustrating, and still baffle many anglers, is that these insects play by a different set of rules. When you see caddis zigzagging up from the surface or swarming upriver in squadrons, you have to do more than change your fly pattern. You need to put on a totally different hat, too, because conventional fly-fishing tactics are based on mayfly behavior patterns.

While it was virtually impossible to buy any caddis imitations twenty-five years ago, at least that problem has been solved. Well-stocked fly shops now offer bin after bin of sunk and floating imitations.

It's what you *do* with these excellent new patterns that makes the difference. No matter how realistic your imitation may be, if you don't know how these insects behave, and duplicate those actions, you're in for slim pickings.

Pupae that leave their cases to hatch out on the surface are a good case in point. They don't drift lazily downstream, gradually rising to the surface, the way most mayfly nymphs do. Nearly all of them zoom to the surface like Poseidon missiles.

This ascent is so rapid that the nimble trout miss nearly half of them. One of the surest signs that fish are taking pupal emergers is the slashing *chug* rise-form of a charging trout. Another is the frequent sight of a caddis fluttering up from the boil, indicating a clean miss.

How can you make your pupal imitation duplicate this violent motion? The best way is to wade directly upstream of a rising fish, making sure to stay out of sight. Make a measuring cast to one side of the fish to get the range, then cast directly at the lie. But, on the foreward pitch, stop the rod abruptly at the vertical. This will make your fly land well short of the fish and dump esses of line on the water in front of you. Your imitation will now sink as it dead-drifts down toward the trout, but, when the line pulls tight, your fly will rise suddenly toward the surface, just like a racing pupa. If your fly is even a fair imitation of the hatching naturals, it will be nearly irresistible.

If the water is too high or the river too deep to allow you to wade upstream of a riser, you're not completely out of the game. There is a "second-best" presentation that will work most of the time.

Position yourself directly across-stream from the fish and cast well above his lie. Let the fly sink as it drifts down and, just as it nears his nose, tighten up suddenly. This will make your fly rise up and start to swing toward you. This motion is nearly as deadly as the one you create with the dead, downstream dump-cast. Needless to say, in both cases, if your fly is weighted or if you've added some lead to your leader, your fly will approach the fish from lower down in the water column and will have a longer and more tempting upward travel.

As a hatch progresses and intensifies, the fish become more familiar with the adults on the surface and will start to take a floating imitation. Since dry-fly fishing is more visual, and hence more fun, I usually switch over to a floater at this point.

Again, the standard upstream dead-drift presentation will attract few, if any, rises. Caddis don't float downstream like stately statues the way mayflies do. Most get off the water as if it were a hot stove.

Trout know this, too. Most caddis will give only a twitch or a shudder or two before taking off. Trout will pounce on any cripples or hatchers the instant they spot them.

Once you've located a good fish that's rising splashily to caddis, wade to a point across from, and slightly above, him. Now, cast to a spot about a foot above his position—preferably with an upstream curve in your line and leader—and jiggle your fly just enough to twinkle it on the surface. This isn't as difficult as it sounds. Your line will be tight as it falls to the surface and a slight movement of your rod tip will transmit the same amount of movement to your fly.

After you've twitched your fly, wobble out extra line through your guides so your fly can drift down over the fish. And it's a good idea to raise your rod tip slightly to cushion the anticipated strike. Trout really belt a dry caddis and, since your line will be nearly taut, something has to give. Better your rod tip than your leader tippet.

There's another presentation, developed by Ernie Maltz, the old wizard of New York's Beaverkill, that often works when caddis are hatching. When Ernie had marked down a regular riser, he would wade into range, false-casting as he went. The next time the fish

rose, he'd drop his fly immediately on the fish's head—right in the center of the rise-form.

Ernie felt this worked because trout miss a lot of emergers and that this instant presentation gave an eager fish a second chance to get even. Perhaps that's true because, the sooner the fly hits the water after the rise, the better it works. However, I reserve this trick for especially difficult trout. Constant false-casting can wear your arm down in a matter of minutes.

Another occasion when trout are vulnerable to a floating caddis imitation is when they return to the stream for egg-laying. Some evening, dense clouds of caddis swarm upstream, some well overhead, but others just above the surface. Unfortunately, all of these won't be egg-layers. Caddis live a couple of weeks or more as adults and join this social evening flight whether or not they're ready for mating.

But enough of them—maybe one out of a dozen—will be ripe and this vast armada of insects, clearly visible overhead, advertises the coming event to the trout. They're alerted and poised to pounce on any insect that dips to the surface to rinse off its eggs.

The drill here is much the same as it is with emergers. Cast across and slightly downstream. However, most egg-layers are more active than hatchers are. Instead of just twinkling your fly, you can give it a pronounced movement, let it float for a couple of feet by paying out line, then twitch it again. Since some species are more active than others, watch the behavior of that evening's flight and manipulate your fly accordingly.

Sometimes this presentation won't work, though, because all species of caddis don't play by the same rules. Some don't deposit their eggs on the water surface. They dive-bomb their way through the rubbery surface tension, swim down with their agile legs, and lay their eggs directly on the cobbles. Others use waterweeds, submerged branches, and deadfalls to crawl down and oviposit on the stream bottom.

Obviously, a surface-twitched caddis isn't going to get much action when underwater egg-layers are the blue-plate special. When you see no rise-forms despite the clouds of returning caddis, that should tip you off.

Few stream-bottom egg-layers make it back to the surface, I've been told. Their mission in life accomplished, and the air bubble they've taken underwater with them exhausted, they soon die and drift downcurrent.

You can still cash in, however, if you tie on an old-fashioned wet fly the size and color of the naturals. Cast this across and slightly upstream to allow the artificial to sink as it dead-drifts during the first part of your presentation. And be sure to fish out the tightline portion of the swing, giving short tugs on the line. Some of these spent flies will be still alive and trying to kick their way back up to the surface.

Of course, all the aforementioned pattern types and presentations can be used for prospecting, or pounding up trout, when you see neither flies nor rise-forms. After all, trout will be equally tempted by the unexpected appearance of a solitary caddis pupa or adult as it will be by the sight of a random mayfly nymph or dun.

There's one more caddis-imitating presentation that's my favorite for teasing up trout. However, this technique works only on pocket water or rather fast sections of streams.

I rerig my terminal tackle, changing to a stouter, streamer-fly leader. To the end of this, I tie on the biggest, bulkiest bucktail I can find. Color or pattern doesn't matter since it will rarely take a fish, anyway. I'm just using it as a drogue to pull my line tight and high above the surface in swift currents.

Some four feet up my leader, just above a leader knot, I tie a dropper fly onto three to four inches of 5-pound-test-plus nylon. The fly I choose is a fat-bodied #10 or #12 with a soft hen hackle or mottled gamebird plumage. This is the killing part of my rig.

I cast this some thirty feet downstream, holding my rod up nearly vertical, feeding out, or taking in, line until the dropper is just skipping on the surface. Now, I'm in business.

To make my fly behave like a hovering or egg-laying caddis, I wiggle my rod tip from side to side as I raise and lower it slightly. This makes the dropper dip in and out of the surface film while it zigzags across the surface.

Since my fly will be skittering and dipping directly downstream from me, I have to wade from side to side to cover all the likely water. And I move very slowly because this presentation is most effective when you tantalize the trout. Dibbling the fly for thirty seconds or more over the choicest spots is no waste of time. I've had large trout savage my fly after it had been playing above their heads for over a minute.

And therein lies the special bonus of fishing caddisfly imitations. When trout tip up and sip in your dun imitation, you certainly feel a solid satisfaction. But when they explode after either your pupal or floating caddis imitation, the sensation is nearer to cardiac arrest. And that turns what used to be termed a "nuisance" into the most exhilarating type of fly fishing there is.

1994

19

The World's Greatest Trout Fisherman

How a French angler, armed with
a Neanderthal cane-pole, catches
a sackful of spooky brown trout.

I have been lucky enough, on rare occasions, to have fished with a few angling superstars such as Art Flick, George Harvey, and Ernie Schwiebert, to drop a few names, and I'll admit I was dazzled and humbled by their streamcraft and rod mastery. Yet even their impressive catches—or, more properly, catch-and-releases—couldn't compare with those of an unknown Frenchman I met briefly some thirty years ago.

This chance encounter took place on the Tarn River in south-central France near the town of Mostuejouls a few miles downstream from the famous and spectacular Gorges du Tarn. The river here is a clear, gentle limestoner some thirty to fifty feet wide and, as the Parisian fly fisher who'd recommended this site had promised, well stocked with decent-sized trout. What he had neglected to tell my wife and me was that these fish were excruciatingly difficult to catch.

Village idlers, vacationers like myself, plus heavy re-enforcements of weekend warriors were keeping the IQs of these trout at artificially high levels. On top of this, they were getting postgraduate courses from a dozen or so professional market fishermen. Any trout that made it to adulthood through this survival course was as jittery as a virgin in a mining-town saloon.

By the way, these professional trouters were absolute magicians with the fly rod. They had to be to stay in business. They caught (and then sold to local inns and restaurants) enough of these ultrasophisticated fish to support their families, without other employment, for five months of each year. I'd have been on welfare within a week. I'm convinced that, granted access, they could have cleaned out both the Test and the Itchen in a fortnight. And yet, I once saw them utterly outclassed—and on their home waters, too.

I eyewitnessed this landmark event shortly after noon on a hot, sunny day in late May. My wife and I were finishing our riverbank picnic when we noticed an odd figure approaching. It was a man about five feet tall, weighing maybe 100 pounds after a big meal, fiftyish, with lots of unruly black hair and a small matching mustache. He was clutching several sections of a whole-cane rod and was sporting the baggiest pair of trousers I'd ever seen outside a burlesque house.

"My God," I whispered to my wife, "This guy's a dead ringer for Charlie Chaplin."

Since we were lounging directly in his path, Charlie stopped to pay his respects. He smiled broadly, bowed, and then uttered something absolutely incomprehensible. Somewhat flustered, I invited him to sit down and join us in my best French, which wasn't too bad in those days. His smile froze, but he didn't sit down and I could see that we were up against an unbreakable language barrier.

We'd been warned that some of the area's inhabitants spoke only patois and Charlie was clearly one of these. The Mostuejouls dialect was apparently one of a kind. It sounded nothing like French, and other patois-speakers only ten miles away complained that they couldn't understand a word of it. Apparently, the Spanish and Italians had left behind many words when they occupied the area during the Middle Ages, and it was rumored that the basic tongue was a pidgin Visigoth. Regardless, this was the only language Charlie seemed to know and we were obviously in for tough sledding if we got into the finer nuances of metaphysics.

I gestured for him to sit down, which he did, and, since we'd just finished all the food, I opened a spare bottle of wine from our hamper and poured him a drink. After a few gulps, he began conversing with vigorous gesticulations, asking me, clearly enough, whether or not I'd had any luck.

Since I'd had a better-than-average morning, I was all too ready to show off the two cleaned eleven-inch trout that lay in our cooler. Charlie nodded respectfully, but I could sense he wasn't overly impressed by this mediocre brace. Nor did he seem a bit inquisitive about our new, lightweight Hardy rods and reels that were propped up against a nearby tree.

This perplexed me because his own gear, by contrast, was barely one step above what you'd expect to see on the walls at Lasceaux. It consisted of three four-foot sections of stout, whole Calcutta bamboo culms fitted with crude, homemade brass ferrules. The tip section was as thick as my thumb and looked unbendable. Wound around the end of his were several feet of what looked like a stout cod-line, ending with a hefty slug of lead, below which hung a small hook on a thick snell.

Since there were also barbel, dace, and chubs in the Tarn, I suspected that one of these coarse fish was his primary catch. To pin things down, I pointed to his rod and, stretching my international vocabulary, asked, in sequence, "Trout?" . . . "Forellen?" . . . "Truchas?" . . . "Truites?"

The last word clicked. He nodded vigorously and wriggled with excitement. Then, borrowing heavily from Marcel Marceau, I made a size indication by opening and closing the gap between my open palms as if playing an imaginary accordion. Charlie quickly responded with a reciprocal gesture indicating a range of twelve to eighteen inches.

I then went to the final deaf-and-dumb question by popping up one finger, then two, and so on up to five to get some inkling of his usual take. He semiphored back "high fives" with both hands three times with a tentative fourth. I was being told that he expected to catch thirty to forty Tarn trout of at least a 1-pound average, and I began to suspect that he'd had a big head start before I'd poured him that glass of wine.

When he'd finished his drink, Charlie stood up, steadily enough, picked up his rod sections and, after a courtly bow to my wife, indicated that I was invited to join his fishing expedition. I turned to my wife and said, "Here it is the middle of a hot, bright day and old Charlie is going to show me how to catch over 30 pounds of Tarn trout on Stone Age tackle. Wild horses couldn't drag me away from this expedition."

"O.K.," she said, opening a paperback. "I'll keep an eye on the rods, but be back in an hour. It's open-air market day in Millau and if we don't run down there before closing time, there's no dinner."

I followed Charlie some two hundred yards upriver to a stretch that was choked with wall-to-wall willow bushes and was considered utterly unfishable from this bank. Charlie gave me a policeman's stop signal when we were about twenty feet from the willows, handed me his rod and left me there while he pussyfooted up to a small chink in the foliage. He peered intently for half a minute then stepped back, held two fingers about eight inches apart and shook his head.

He tiptoed up to the next gap and, after a few seconds, nodded enthusiastically with his hands spread about sixteen inches apart. He joined me, took back the tip-section of his rod and then reached dramatically into his baggy pants pocket. With a flourish, out came a small plastic box crammed full of Hornets, wasps, and large blue-bottle flies. Confined to such cramped, suffocating quarters, this miniature zoo was as angry as hell and said so with a noise that sounded like a rattlesnake.

Charlie popped open the lid, snatched a wasp by the wings, and snapped it shut again before the bugs could realize that liberation was at hand. He quickly stuck the hook through the wasp's thorax and, again gesturing me to stay put, sneaked back to his peephole.

He wound up line so the wasp was snug to the rod tip and gingerly threaded some three feet of the pole through the foliage. Then, with a rapid rotating motion, lowered the bait to the water surface where he dapped and dibbled the buzzing insect.

In a few seconds, I heard a healthy splash, Charlie jerked the rod and began rolling up line as fast as he could and backed away slowly until a thrashing trout, nose tight up against the pole, emerged from the bushes. Charlie rejoined me, unhooked the trout, whacked it on the head with a stout rod-section and dropped it into the gunnysack that was draped around his neck.

After he'd baited up again, he entrusted me with his bait supply as well as his extra rod-sections and stalked back to the wall of willows. I followed him at a discreet interval, realizing I'd been awarded the trusted position of ghillie. A bit later, I was granted the further honor of lugging his gunnysack, which had become heavy enough to hamper his activities.

As I grew more familiar with Charlie's tactics, it dawned on me that they were murderously ingenious. He was managing to duck the discomforts of dawn patrols or stumbling around after sunset by plying his trade in the middle of the day when other anglers were home taking a siesta.

Of course, all Tarn anglers, professional or amateur, knew that when the sun got high, the trout deserted the midstream currents for the shady overhang along the banks. But what they didn't know— and Charlie did—was how to haul them out of those sanctuaries.

No one using a conventional fly rod stood a chance of taking those jungle-dwellers. Even if lucky enough to get a fly down to the water surface, there was no way an angler using fly tackle could get a trout back out of that maze of twigs and branches with a fine leader and whippy rod tip.

Charlie's paleolithic rig was tailor-made for this task, though. His heavy-wire #12 hook wasn't so large that it would disfigure the bug impaled on it yet it had enough gape to secure a firm grip on a trout's jaw. The short, stout snell—it looked about 8-pound test— never touched the water and so was unlikely to be noticed by a trout focused on the bouncing insect, yet it was plenty strong enough to derrick up a thrashing trout of several pounds. The heavy sinker and stiff line were needed to make sure the baited hook kept on ricocheting off twigs and branches until the bait finally reached pay dirt. And the stiff rod, operated on the principle of a roller-curtain, needs no justification. So much for "fine and far off."

Every minute or two—rarely as long as three—Charlie would bring over a flopping fish and pick out another bait. He rarely resorted to using two sections of his rod, and the third seemed reserved for whacking trout between the eyes. He did lose the odd fish to the dense foliage, but he won about four bouts out of five.

The sack was getting really heavy by the time my wife located us. She was impatient to take off, but I insisted she spend a few minutes to watch Charlie's drill.

Sensing we were about to leave, Charlie put down his rod and came over to smile, bow, and shake hands. I thought we would run across him again in the weeks ahead, but, unfortunately, we never did.

During our run down to Millau, the full significance of that fishing episode began to dawn on me.

"Do you realize that Charlie caught twenty, maybe twenty-five, trout in about an hour? All smart, grown-up fish that must have added up to well over 30 pounds? And out of the Tarn?"

"Did he really catch that many?"

"You saw his gunnysack. I'll bet you'd have had trouble just lifting it. Why, he's probably the best fisherman in this valley—perhaps in all France. What am I saying? He's probably the greatest trout fisherman in the whole world!"

To put an end to my babbling, my wife said, "I'm surprised that a purist like you is so impressed with a lowly live-bait fisher."

"You're being too hard on the great man," I argued. "I'll admit that wasps and hornets fall into the live-bait category. But, when he put on a blue-bottle, he was definitely fishing with a fly, wasn't he?"

1989

20

What to Do When There's No Hatch to Match

Glut hatches are becoming increasingly rare.
Here's how to pound up trout
when there's not a dimple in sight.

I have never met a fly fisher who didn't hope, or even pray, for a good hatch of flies when he headed for his favorite river or stream. Flies on the water nearly always mean productive fishing. Rise-forms reveal the exact positions of trout and, because they're obviously on the feed, all you have to do is to come up with the matching artificial and present it drag-free. This is, unquestionably, the most visual and therefore, the most exciting, type of fishing.

Unfortunately, there are often hours on end—sometimes even entire days—when you don't see a single fly on the water, not even the odd one fluttering in the air. Which fly do you tie on then? And how do you fish it?

If you happen to be on a limestoner or spring creek, my advice is to sit, watch, and wait. I have never had much success blind-fishing on such streams with either a dry fly or a nymph. The trout seem to hide under clumps of weeds and take a snooze until hatching flies wake them up. However, these placid, weed-paved streams are enormously rich in insect life and you shouldn't have too long a wait until at least a few flies appear and you can go to work over a rising fish or two.

But over 95 percent of our trout streams are freestoners that are much less generous. Once the main, spring hatches are over, flies can become scarce. When you hit a dead period, or even a hatchless full day, you are faced with two choices. You can head back to your car and go home or you can take up the challenge and start prospecting.

If the water happens to be a bit high and, perhaps, roiley, you don't need a Ph.D. in aquatic biology to know what to do. You should swing a streamer across and downstream, and the dirtier the water, the brighter your fly should be. A Yellow Marabou or a Mickey Finn are my cloudy-water favorites.

One of the most skillful streamer-fishers I know recently gave me a tip on how to take a big trout once you've pinpointed his lie. Wade out about forty feet above the fish and tie on your largest streamer. Cast directly in front of him, then slowly swing your rod, right and left, playing the fly in front of his nose.

Trout, especially large ones, are fiercely territorial and won't suffer little ones to enter their zone—especially into the feed-lane in front of them. Even though the fish may not be totally convinced that your fly is, indeed, a real live fish, he will become annoyed at its infringement. His anger will build and often, after several minutes of goading, he'll take the law into his own hands. Fortunately for you, he has no hands and has to use his mouth!

It's when water is at normal, or distinctly low, levels that you face the most difficult decisions. Without any visual clues, you have to conjure up what size and color of fly a trout might be willing to take and in which water layer he might expect to find it.

About the only guidance you'll get on these questions will come from that day's weather pattern. If the day seems near perfect (even though the aquatic insects don't seem to agree) your prospects are fairly good. A blue sky or one with only an occasional puffy cloud and crisp, low-humidity air are sure signs of a high barometer. In this kind of weather you feel friskier and trout do, too.

On such days, once the sun has burned off the early morning chill, your chances are good even though no, or very few, flies appear. Though the trout may not be showing due to the lack of naturals, they will be hovering on the fin, in a mood to feed. It's your job now to give them a good reason to do so.

Since the fish are in a receptive mood, you can fish for them the easy way: with the dry fly. But forget your springtime, #14 Quill Gordons, Hendricksons, and Light Cahills. Offer them a mouthful big enough to make their trip to the surface seem worth the effort.

By far the most effective prospecting fly I've ever used is Art Flick's Gray Fox Variant. There seems to be a special magic in the blend of ginger and grizzly hackle—a feature it shares with that all-time favorite, the Adams.

There's no need to tie on one of those huge #10 powder puffs that are so difficult to cast. I find the #14s with a hackle-diameter not much larger than a silver half-dollar do the job nicely.

I like to alter my variants a bit by cutting a 45-degree "V" out of the hackle-collar just in front of the hook point. These lowest fibers pierce the water surface, anyway, and don't help flotation. Then, too, this pruned fly is less wind-resistant, cocks hook-down more often, and its long hackle-fibers are less likely to snag in the bend of the hook.

A dun variant of similar size is my second choice. I've found that if I give my variants a tiny tug—just enough to twinkle them in the surface film—as they approach a hot spot, my batting average improves.

There are several other dry flies that are good choices for pounding up trout. A chunky #10 Irresistible makes a buoyant floater that's a meaty mouthful.

Inch-long, yellow-bodied grasshopper imitations often work well, too, for the same reasons. While virtually no grasshoppers plop into my home river—99 percent of its banks are tree-lined—the trout probably mistake it for a giant, golden stonefly, a few of which are seen fluttering around all summer long. I find the patterns with clipped deer-hair bodies float best.

There's one more fly you should add to your list and it, too, is a land insect: a large, floating black ant. For some reason, trout are inordinately fond of ants. George Harvey, the Pennsylvania sage, ties a slightly oversized pattern on a #10 hook out of black deer-hair which makes an excellent floater.

I'll have to admit that I've never seen an ant quite that big. Even the common, juicy carpenter ant isn't larger than #14. But the shiny black surface and distinctive wasp waist telegraph "ant" to the trout, and George swears that the big pattern pulls up more trout than a smaller one does. Perhaps it's much like the case for oversized duck decoys. Some experienced waterfowlers are convinced they pull in more birds than regular ones do.

George's home waters are the slow meadowland streams of central Pennsylvania where most of our terrestrial patterns were developed, so you could expect him to be partial to ants. However, I've found this pattern to be killing on mountain streams, as well.

On the bleaker side, when there's a heavy cloud layer or, even worse, drizzle or rain, you'll probably be hard-pressed to take even a few trout. I, personally, have never enjoyed good fishing under such conditions. Rotten weather is a sure sign of a low, or falling, barometer and low readings almost always mean stingy catches. Somehow, they put the fish off their feed and send them to the sullen stream bottom.

Even so, don't head for your car to go home. After all, a few trout are better than none. And don't take heart in the forecast for bluebird weather on Monday, a day or two from now. You're on the stream *today* and you'd better make the most of it because, by Monday, you'll be back in the old salt mine, won't you?

To catch any fish at all under bad-weather conditions, you'll have to fish like an opening-day wormer, trying to bang the fish on the nose with your fly. This calls for either a well-weighted nymph or a split-shot or two on your leader. Neither rig is a joy to cast, but some days this is the only game in town.

Unless you're on a large, deep river like Montana's Missouri or New York's Delaware, you can rake bottom with a floating line. Cast a well-weighted nymph upstream and take in line at current speed as your fly sinks and drifts back toward you.

One of my favorite patterns for this type of fishing is an over-sized, yellow stonefly nymph. Those tied on 3X-long hooks in sizes #8 or #10 give room on the hook shank for plenty of lead under the seal's fur dubbing. A Light Cahill or Black Woolly Bugger of similar size and heft are good choices, too.

On smaller, shallower streams, a #12 Hare's Ear Nymph is hard to beat and the old Leadwing Coachman is a close second. If these patterns in your fly box aren't weighted, be sure to add a little lead to your leader.

When upstream nymphing, you'll be able to cover very little water at the proper depth so make every shot count. If you're on familiar water, concentrate on the known, best lies. When you're on a strange stream, stick to deep runs, pocket-water, or areas where the chop slows up at the head of a pool.

This style of fishing calls for excruciating concentration on your leader or strike-indicator to detect the slight movement that signals a strike. When I find my attention span failing, every hour or less, I spell myself with another deep-fishing method.

I change reel-spools to a line with a fast-sinking tip and cast up and across-stream. Until the line gets below me, the fly sinks deeply and then arcs downcurrent. This switchover takes less than a minute and the presentation, though less killing, covers far more water.

Perhaps the deadliest deep-fishing technique of them all is to make your fly behave like an emerging caddis-pupa. While this presentation covers the least water of all—not much more than a square foot—it may be the most irresistible one to a precisely located trout.

This method is simply a vigorous variation of the "Leisenring Lift." Pennsylvania's Big Jim Leisenring was considered by many the best wet-fly fisherman of his generation.

This method, and a variation on it, are described in greater detail on pages 166–67. It's hard to imagine a better way to imitate a mayfly nymph that's swimming up to hatch out.

Fortunately for us trout fishers, the fly rod is the most versatile piece of fishing tackle yet invented. It offers so many differing styles and patterns of flies and so many presentation techniques that only floods or freeze-ups should dictate fishless days. Even when no flies—or only a few stragglers—appear, there's always a chance of taking fish.

I recall one blustery day in early May last year. It was cloudy, windy, and there were even a few brief snow flurries. I fished a nymph deep and doggedly for three miserable hours during the early afternoon. I landed two browns in the 12″-to-14″ range plus a plump brookie that stretched to nearly 11 inches.

Definitely not a catch to send one running to the taxidermist. But, looking back on last season now, the taking of those three lovely trout, with the odds stacked so strongly against me, makes that day the one I remember most vividly.

1994

1

Little Tricks
That Take
Summer Trout

Midsummer trout aren't on the lookout
for dead-drift duns. You need new ties
and tactics to tempt them.

The average dry-fly fisherman is about as well-equipped to fool summer trout as a golfer would be to win the U.S. Open with a bag full of putters. In any sport you're handicapped when you limit yourself to just one aspect of the game.

All those patterns, sizes, and colors you see in fly boxes don't mean real variety to a trout because most of the flies will be the same shape. The reason for this is that over 99 percent of the dry flies sold today—from minute midges to galumphing #8s—have an identical silhouette. Their sweeping tails, slim bodies, and upright wings show that they're an imitation of some type of mayfly and, unfortunately, mayflies are only an occasional snack for summer trout.

Mayflies may well have been the staple diet of the trout on the stately chalkstreams of southern England where dry-fly fishing was developed over eighty years ago. These privileged streams are spring-fed, have a relatively stable year-round temperature, and an even volume of flow—conditions that are ideal for this fragile type of aquatic insect. But trout on our eastern up-and-down, hot-and-cold, semipolluted waters have been forced to turn to more plebeian fare to fill their bellies.

The original dry-fly drill, as it was proclaimed by a Victorian gentleman named Frederick M. Halford, laid down the law for all right-thinking anglers with no ifs, ands, or buts. First you found a trout that was feeding on mayflies that had hatched out on the surface and were floating down on the gentle current. Next you tied on an exact (or nearly exact) imitation of that specific species of fly. This you pitched upstream of your quarry, letting it float back over him dead-drift (or as if it were completely unattached) until he accepted it as one of the naturals.

Any attempt to cater to the fish's anger, curiosity, or greed was simply not done. A gentleman abided by the code or he was shunned. Many fishermen who kept on casting the vulgar sunk-fly in those days were asked to resign from their fishing club!

Despite the ultraliberated attitudes we pride ourselves on today, the fraternity of dry-fly fishermen may be the last stronghold of corsetted Victorianism. Our dry flies and our methods of fishing them are unflinchingly nineteenth century. This despite the fact that entomologists, and the proof-positive stomach contents of our trout, tell us that trout in America today make far more meals on the three other orders of insects that hatch off the water and on random land-bred insects than they do on Halford's hallowed mayflies. In light of this, casting a repertoire consisting only of artificial mayflies at our trout is about as realistic as Marie Antoinette's advice for the starving peasants: "Let them eat cake."

Our method of presenting these flies is no less archaic than our selection of patterns. Watch a pool when only a few flies are floating down, and you'll see what I mean. Insects that make the trip with quiet resignation travel a long way before, or if, they are taken. But the ones that skitter, flutter, or struggle are gone in a wink.

I have proved this point to myself time and again by capturing a small supply of assorted insects and positioning myself upstream from a good fishing spot. If I kill the insects before dropping them into the current, they usually pass over the fish's lies unmolested. But when I pitch them, alive and kicking, into the same feed lane they are regularly taken with a resounding smack. There's little question about it: The moving fly draws the rise as surely as the squeaky wheel gets the grease.

It's true that an accurate imitation of a natural fly fished in a free-floating manner may be taken—and taken readily—when trout are rising regularly to a particular species of fly. But what about all those hours when trout aren't actively feeding? Will a totally unexpected fly with some fifty extra legs, too many tails, and a great hook hanging down below it seem real enough to pull a wary trout up off the bottom? Or will he class it with the twigs, berries, hemlock needles, and leaf-cuttings that also drift over his lie all day long? The latter is usually the case as most of us know from sad experience. Under these conditions, your imitation needs something extra going for it if you are going to convince the trout that your counterfeit is, indeed, alive.

To catch a loafing trout's attention and to gain his confidence, your fly should move as a living insect does. This means a small movement, not a great plowing wake. And it should move in an *upstream* direction. For all stream-bred flies, whether hatching out or returning for egg laying, move in an upcurrent direction. If this were not so, if each generation of winged adults did not leapfrog upstream, floods would have rolled all the underwater larvae downstream eons ago, and all our aquatic insects would have died in the brine of the Atlantic or Pacific oceans.

The reason any motion to the dry fly has been damned for decades is not that natural flies don't move, but that when the fisherman cast his fly upcurrent, as doctrine dictated, any motion except for a free drift was either downstream, across-stream, or both. These were behavior patterns so unrealistic and alarming that they sent all but the most calloused trout scurrying for cover.

If, on the other hand, you break with tradition and cast your fly in an across and downstream direction, when you give it a tiny twitch it will lurch upstream. Then let it float free again as long as it will. That small motion is enough to catch the trout's attention and tell him that your offering is, indeed, alive and edible. Gently does it, though. The game is like calling ducks. Overdo it, and you defeat your own ends.

This slightly moved dry fly is the only way I've ever been able to raise trout consistently when they're in a lethargic mood during the summer months and there are no big fly hatches to keep them feeding regularly on the surface. This method will even raise good fish out of deep slow water at midday when only mad dogs and Englishmen would think of being astream.

There's only one problem with this seemingly unorthodox system. You probably haven't a fly in your box that will keep floating, and floating high, after you've given it that tantalizing twitch. Those few wispy tail feathers on the average mayfly imitation are asked to float two-thirds of the hook weight while all that hackle up at the head holds up the easy one-third. Break the precarious hold this tail has gained on the surface tension and down goes the bottom half of your fly. The appearance of the floating remains is too unrealistic for even the most freshly stocked trout.

Then too, the mayfly silhouette—even if this type of fly occasionally remained afloat—doesn't look like most midsummer insects. It has long tails, is basically translucent, and has upright wings. The other important insects that emerge from the water, such as caddisflies, stoneflies, true flies, and nearly all insects that are blown onto the water from the neighboring land have no tails or very small ones, wings that lie along the top of, or to the sides of, the body, and are basically opaque.

Cut open the next trout you catch on a midsummer afternoon (if you can take one on a standard fly) and examine the stomach contents carefully. I'm sure that what you'll find there would make Halford whirl in his grave like a #10 fan-wing cast on a gossamer 8X tippet. Ants, wasps, bees, crane flies, beetles, and houseflies will form the bulk and, if there are any aquatic insects in the mix, there will probably be as many caddisflies and stoneflies as there are mayflies. If you'll take a trout stomach's word for what he's been eating, you'll have to ask yourself the agonizing question: "What do I match when there's no hatch?"

This is a question you'll have to answer for a greater part of the day over a longer portion of the season in the years ahead, for good hatches of mayflies are disappearing on most of our waters. They are already a great rarity on most northeastern waters after June 1, and really profuse hatches earlier in the season are becoming infrequent enough to be talked about again and again as major events.

Caddis hatches, on the other hand, seem to be as heavy as ever and stoneflies, the third most important order of aquatic insects, seem to be holding their own, too. Apparently, both of these types of insects are tougher and more tolerant of the flooding, heating, and polluting that progress brings to our running waters.

Yet perhaps the most important part of the trout's diet during mid and late summer is made up of the wide variety of land-bred insects that fall onto the water. Grasshoppers and beetles have long been recognized as trout delicacies, and good imitations are available at many tackle stores. But what about the other windfalls that trout feed on during hot weather?

The observant fishermen in Pennsylvania's limestone country have come up with ingenious imitations of the leafhoppers, Japanese beetles, and tiny ants that fall onto their waters. But little attention has been paid to the corresponding insects that tumble into woodland streams at this time of year. Terrestrial insects are equally important to mountain trout as they are to fish inhabiting meadow streams flowing through rich agricultural areas, but they are a very different-looking collection.

In an attempt to fill this important, though empty, corner of our fly boxes, I have experimented with a series of prototypes that cover most of the insects I find on mountain streams and inside trout during midsummer. You should certainly enlarge on and vary this selection by copying insect types you find most frequently in your area. All these flies, despite their apparent differences in size, shape, and color have one characteristic in common. They are the most buoyant artificials I have ever fished with. They will ride high and cocky on the surface even after they have been twitched smartly.

In case you're a fly tyer, or have a friend who will tie for you, you may be interested in how they are made. They are no more difficult to produce than standard patterns, but there are a few tricks that may make your first attempts easier. This series of flies, for tying purposes, can be separated into three broad types that are different in small but important ways.

Caddisflies are one of the choicest trout foods during the big daytime hatches of spring and during their usual flights at dusk all summer long. But, equally important, they are excellent general patterns for prospecting or for trying to pound up fish that aren't surface feeding at the moment. I have found dark gray, brown, and ginger-and-grizzly-mixed the most productive colors, and I like them in sizes #12, #14, and #16. Larger flies might seem to be a better mouthful to an uncommitted trout, but I have found that bigger hooks are usually too heavy for optimum flotation. Smaller #18s and #20s, on the other hand, present the trout with too small an inducement to be worth the perilous trip all the way to the surface.

To tie this fly, start with a body of the same color as the wings and hackle of the finished imitation and wind it onto the rear half of the hook shank only. Keep this body extremely thin, because the wing—which you are going to tie on next—must lie parallel to the shank, and a fat body would make the wing fibers flair up and out at an angle that would spoil the tight, realistic silhouette of your pattern.

Now select a long-fibered hackle feather of top quality—the sort you would usually reserve for tails of mayfly imitations—even-up the tips of the fibers and twitch off a section about three-quarters of an inch wide. Tie this in directly on top of the body and, if the latter has been kept slim, these wing fibers should lie nearly parallel to the shank and body. Be sure to make the wings twice as long as the body or about the same length as the entire hook. Repeat this process twice more, only tie in the second and third batches of hackle on either side of the hook shank so that the wing surrounds the body on three sides, veiling it as the caddis's wings do. Now taper the wing butts carefully with your scissors to a fine point, tapering toward the eye of the hook. Tie in two good hackles of the size you would use for a conventional fly on that hook size, wind them on, and finish in the usual manner. The completed fly, if tied with suitable materials, should float like duck down and last a long time.

Stonefly imitations are made in much the same way except for slight variations in both the body and the wing. Stonefly bodies should be more succulent, should be colored yellow, brown, or an alternating pattern of the two. Ostrich herl is a good choice here since it gives a chunky appearance without adding much real bulk. This wing, too, should be twice the body length and placed on top of the hook only instead of on top and along the sides. Use light gray or pale dun hackle since these are the usual stonefly wing colors. Hackle at the head should be the same size as you would use for the caddis and wound on in the same manner, but choose a shade that matches the body rather than the wing color. The above suggestions cover the great majority of stoneflies you'll see on mountain streams, but, by all means, imitate any other color combinations you see regularly.

Crane flies, houseflies, wasps, bees, and flying ants are the easiest of all to tie. Start with a good, meaty body colored to match the species in question. You won't have to stint here because you'll want the wings to flair on these flies. Here again use pale dun or grizzly hackle fibers, keeping them the same length as before, but positioning them on the sides of the hook shank only. The finished wings should flair out to the sides at an angle of about 30 degrees the way a bee's or houseflies' wings do. These outriggers of steely hackle will not only make your fly ride high but will help it sit squarely, hook down, every time you cast it. Finish these flies as you would the stonefly imitations, with two conventional hackles suggesting body, rather than wing, color.

These summer flies will float twice as well as standard mayfly imitations if you tie them with the same quality of hackle. The only trouble is that you'll be using a lot more long-fibered hackle which is often hard to get in first-rate quality. Substitute hair whenever you can get good water-repellent guard hairs of the right color. Mink tail is excellent and is produced by breeders in a wide variety of shades. Beaver gives a good dark brown. Woodchucks tail, even though the animal isn't aquatic, sheds water beautifully. So does moose mane. Be careful with deer tail, though. Some portions are useful, but most of it is hollow and will flair badly when tied to the hook.

Admittedly, these patterns are not exact imitations of the flies you'll find in midsummer trout. But they are very appealing *impressions* of these windfall insects, and fish aren't highly selective at this time of year because they don't often see large enough quantities of the same insect to get psychologically imprinted with an exact size, shape, and color. The trick is to give them the *sort* of fly they've been taking and to present it as a struggling, but sitting, duck.

On some afternoons one fly will be preferred; on others a different one will pull more trout to the surface. Experiment, but be guided in your first choice by what you see in the air and on the water. Crane flies often hover and dance over the surface, and an imitation can be deadly when you see a few yo-yoing over a pool. Always be on the alert for a flight of ants, especially when it is hot and sunny.

You may wonder why I tie my flying-ant imitations in this manner since it is well known that these insects usually ride flush in the surface film, rather than high and dry like streambred insects. The answer is that when flying ants fall on the water during midsummer afternoons there are likely to be so many of them that your artificial stands only a fractional chance of being taken unless it advertises itself as a newcomer by its activity. A standard ant can't take the twitch and remain floating while this pattern can. I've found that the twitched imitation will outfish the low-riding, dead-drift one by a wide margin, especially when there are a dozen or more ants per square foot of water.

Above all, when you're prospecting with these flies on a mid-summer morning or afternoon, spray or anoint your fly liberally and change it at the first hint of sogginess. In this type of fishing a half-drowned fly is useless.

Why do I continue to fish the dry fly during the dog days—and hours—when nothing seems to be rising? Why don't I turn to the upstream, dead-drift nymph that so many authors recommend for these conditions? There are three reasons, and any single one of them would be enough to keep me fishing on the surface.

First, upstream nymphing is the most demanding and least diverting kind of trout fishing I've ever tied. It takes far more judgment and concentration to fish an unseen nymph upcurrent without any drag than it does to fish the dry fly in this manner. There's no visible fly to help you regulate your rate of retrieve or to tell you when to strike, either. I find this technique cruel and unusual punishment unless the fish are taking readily. A half hour without a hit is the outside limit of my attention span.

Second, I think it's harder to deceive a trout with a nymph than it is with a dry fly. A floating fly has to be glimpsed through the distorting prisms that hackle fibers set up in the surface tension, giving the trout a blurred view. A nymph, on the other hand, is seen directly through the clear water and any imperfections stand out sharply, which is probably the reason wet flies and nymphs work best only in fast or turbulent currents.

But the third and main reason the dry fly, properly fished, will beat the sunk fly under low-water conditions is that the surface carries most of the insect food at this time of year. The stream bed may be teeming with nymphs, but they hide under rocks during the day and crawl out only at dusk or after dark. Summertime aquatic insects rarely swim up to emerge till late evening, and even then they may be pitifully few in number. The main food supply most of the day is made up of insects that have flown or tumbled onto the surface, and these, trapped in the rubbery surface film, are carried downstream on top of the water. Sample the drift food in a stream at this time of year with a cheesecloth net, and you'll find that the middle and lower layers of the current yield almost no food at all.

For all of these reasons, then, you can presume that daytime feeding fish are expecting their food on the surface. This is fortunate for the angler, for here his fly stands the best chance of both catching the fish's attention and preventing him from getting too close a look at the imitation.

1974

22

The Alive-and-Kicking Dry Fly

We tend to consider trout as dainty sippers,
but they're really slashing carnivores.
Here's how to trigger this instinct.

I'm now convinced that the traditional method of fishing the dry fly is all wet. It pains me to say this about the most beautiful and hallowed method of angling: I'm one of the millions who have been fascinated by it for years. But I am now almost certain that fishing the conventional dry fly in a dead-drift manner is dead wrong most of the time on most of our streams.

Not that the floating fly itself is dead—or even dying. Far from it. In fact, I'm predicting new life for the dry fly because more and more fishermen, as they examine the evidence, will begin to fish the floating fly as an alive-and-kicking insect instead of presenting it as a bunch of dead feathers.

I have been a confirmed heretic about both our standard patterns and our conventional ways of fishing them ever since one late-May morning several years ago when I met the perfect fly fisherman. I first sighted him some one hundred yards downstream and, even at that distance, his casting and presentation seemed so elegant that I sat down on a boulder out of respect and watched him work up the pool. When he reached the white water that marked the top of that stretch, he reeled in and walked over toward me, giving an informal greeting with his hand.

"Any luck?" I asked.

He shook his head. "I've raised only one and he was bait-sized. I didn't expect to do much till late afternoon, anyway, but it's just too great a day to be sitting around the house, isn't it?" Then he wished me luck and walked off slowly upstream and I never even found out what his name was.

I rested the water several minutes and then stepped in—even though his was a hard act to follow. I messed up my first few presentations trying to imitate his crisp, high backcast, then I settled into my normal fishing rhythm and twenty minutes later, when I reached the bottom of the pool, I realized I had raised seven trout and landed four—two of which had been twelve-inchers and very respectable fish for those waters.

Admittedly, I'm not considered a duffer—I manage to put in fifty to sixty days on trout waters each season and have for years—but I wouldn't dream of classing myself with the unknown angler who'd preceded me. Yet I had interested far more fish despite his obvious advantage in streamsmanship. Clearly, the difference in our results was due to another factor: he had been casting a standard pattern in the classic, upstream manner, while I had been fishing a new type of floater downcurrent with a highly unorthodox technique.

The perfect fisherman had made each of his presentations flawlessly—by the book. And the book clearly states that the floating fly must approach and pass over the waiting trout dead-drift or drag-free—meaning that the line and leader must in no way impede the fly from floating downcurrent as if it were a completely detached object. Accomplishing this is no mean feat. Casting upstream with carefully executed curves or waves in the line gives the best chance for success, and the ability to outwit the hidden hands in the current is the accepted measure of a dry-fly man's skill.

I, on the other hand, had been breaking two great dry-fly commandments. I had been fishing in a slightly downstream direction. And I had made my fly move, on purpose, just before it reached the likeliest taking place on each and every cast.

There was a method in my madness, though—a method I'd worked out several years previously after a series of frustrating experiences. On several occasions in close succession I had failed to catch—or even raise—a single fish even though trout were leaping and splashing all around me. And, on each of these occasions, the trout had been feeding on caddisflies that were hatching out and swarming all over the water surface.

These common, but much-neglected, aquatic insects very definitely do not float downcurrent like priceless objects of art. They bounce, crawl, skitter, flutter, and zigzag when on the surface, and always in an upstream direction. Book or no book, I decided, if I were going to catch trout on the dry fly during a caddis hatch, I would have to give my fly some motion and I would have to move it in an upstream direction.

The method I used is the cast described on pages 185–86. My theory is that the tiny twitch I give my fly telegraphs to the waiting trout that a lively caddis is coming downstream, and the trout seem to think so, too.

I soon became so fascinated with this type of presentation that I tried it at odd times of day when no fish were rising. And, to my surprise, I discovered that the twitched caddis was a dual-purpose weapon: it not only did great execution during the previously baffling caddis hatches, but it was a deadly way to pound up fish during those long hours when a few or no fish were showing at the surface.

Further observation soon showed me why this minimanipulation of the fly raised trout when most of them weren't having any. A fluttering fly not only advertises itself more vigorously to a nonfeeding trout, but it is also more realistic since most aquatic insects—whether mayflies, caddisflies, or stoneflies—flutter on the surface before taking off or floating downcurrent.

Once I realized this simple fact, I began to cash in on it with both the fish and the fishermen. While a fishing companion and I would munch soggy sandwiches during the noontime lull, I would start laying bets on the fates of the few straggling insects that occasionally floated downstream. When I spotted a fly struggling on the surface some fifty feet upstream I'd say, "Bet you a quarter a fish takes that fly before he floats down opposite us." And, just to mix it up, I'd bet the opposite way on a fly that was floating downstream inert. Naturally some of the flies crossed me up. Active ones often took off before they reached us and lifeless ones suddenly became active and sealed their own fates. But despite these occasional setbacks, I'd be rich and retired by now if I hadn't run out of takers. Trout preference for a fluttering fly is that predictable.

By this time you're probably wondering: if trout really prefer a surface fly fished with some life to it, why have so many seemingly intelligent men fished the standard floating fly drag-free for so long? After all, many leaders in business, science, and the arts (not to mention two of the last seven presidents of the U.S.) have been dedicated fly fishers. Have they all been duped and deluded?

The answer, I think, lies somewhere between "Yes" and "Probably." And the reason why such a thing could happen in this age of enlightenment makes a fascinating, though little-known, story.

Dry-fly fishing may have been developed over many years by many men, but it didn't reach the angling world at large till 1886. In that year, *Floating Flies and How to Dress Them* was published, and anglers haven't recovered from its enormous influence to this day. The author was Frederick M. Halford, an English gentleman, who gave up money-grubbing in all its forms at a relatively early age to devote his life to the nobler ideals of dry-fly fishing for trout.

The streams Halford fished are the most fertile in the world. The Test and Itchen in southern England produce twenty times as much trout food per cubic foot of water, as do most famous streams on this side of the Atlantic. Back in Halford's fishing days, before road-washings, insecticides, and other pollutants had begun to take

their toll, the hatches of insects, especially of mayflies, on these waters were incredibly profuse.

Under these conditions, a few fish rose fairly steadily all day long, and for several special hours every day when the glut hatches occurred, every fish in the river seemed to be on the take. It was a fly fisher's paradise and too perfect to be spoiled for other club members by some heavy-handed chap who put down the fish by flailing a team of wet flies through these clear waters in the hope of taking an unseen trout.

The accepted drill was quite specific. First a rising trout must be located. Then an accurate imitation of the fly on the water—not just some attractive and buggy looking artificial—must be cast upstream of the trout and allowed to float, dead-drift, over the nose of that particular fish. No attempt must be made to cater to its greed or curiosity. The only proper way to take such fish is to convince them that your counterfeit is, indeed, just another of the duns on which they have been feeding with confidence.

Fishermen on both sides of the Atlantic became fascinated by the science, skill, and delicacy of this new method. Halford became the high priest of a cult that spread the true doctrine with fanatical zeal. Soon the wet fly was considered a secret vice and club members caught using it were asked to resign their expensive rod privileges. The dry fly became a moral issue. After all, dammit, a gentleman didn't shoot grouse on the ground, he didn't cheat at cards, and he most certainly did not fish the wet fly, either!

From what I read, we seem to have shaken off most of our old Victorian hang-ups by this time, but the dry fly is still considered holier than the wet and the Halfordian dogma of dead-drift seems to be a vestigial part of this ethical package. The moral origins of this doctrine may be lost in history, as far as most anglers are concerned, but the ritual is still with us.

In all fairness to Halford, though, I must repeat that he was fishing the stately chalkstreams of southern England, which teem with small mayflies. And even so, he included five highly realistic caddis patterns in his final selection of forty-three dry-fly patterns. But can we, who fish rivers that are mostly rain-fed, acid, and where caddis rival the mayflies for top place on the trout's menu, afford to ignore caddis imitations completely?

For we seem to be doing just that. For example, check the contents of your own dry-fly boxes. How many floating imitations of caddisflies do you carry? Don't count nondescripts or flies like the Adams that are said to duplicate some caddis but are tied with the characteristic mayfly upwings and tails. I mean true caddis patterns like the English "sedges" with wings tied parallel to their bodies and that show a realistic caddis silhouette. Can you find many—or even any—in your fly boxes?

If you're like most anglers I know or meet—and many of these are advanced fly fishers—you probably don't have a single one. And chances are you can't find any at your favorite tackle shop, either.

With the exception of a few terrestrials, nearly all floaters displayed in even the most fully stocked stores are designed to imitate some mayfly or other.

Admittedly, these popular mayfly patterns have proved themselves over and over again—*when there are enough mayflies hatching to start trout feeding regularly and selectively.* But how much of the time do you meet these conditions on the rivers you fish? What do you offer when caddisflies are hatching out in large numbers and trout are feeding on them selectively? What fly do you put on when stoneflies are on the water? Or during those all-too-long periods when nothing is hatching and the trout are taking only the occasional, windfall, land-bred insects like bees, wasps, or houseflies? Is the traditional mayfly silhouette the most appealing to trout at times like these?

I think not. And I think this is the reason why the series of flies I have worked out to represent the most common species of caddisflies have proved themselves as excellent prospecting flies, too. Their silhouettes are more accurate representations of most land-bred windfall insects than are the shapes of the standard mayfly patterns.

Straw, ginger, brown, light dun, dark dun, and ginger-and-grizzly mixed have proved the most useful colors, but there are endless variations. Sizes 16 and 14 seem to cover most common caddis hatches, although I always carry some 18s and 12s just in case. Most of the caddis patterns I use have wings, hackle, and body of the same shade because caddisflies tend to be much the same color all over. My stonefly imitations, tied in the same manner, usually show more contrast, as do the naturals.

If you tie your own flies, or have a friend who ties for you, you may be interested in how these new Fluttering Caddisflies, stoneflies, and terrestrials are tied. A full description appears on pages 188–190.

Each of these patterns represents a larger-than-average investment in choice materials and in effort, but it's worth it in the long run. If properly tied, it will float higher and take more punishment than any other dry fly in your box. And, I've found, it will take more fish, too.

Even if you're not a tyer, or don't know any, you should be able to give these new patterns a tryout next year because several tackle companies tell me they're going to offer this series of flies soon.

I know this is not the perfect dry fly for every single situation although I, myself, now use it the majority of the time. Of course, I still fish standard mayfly imitations when those naturals are on the water—though I often give even these easily sinkable patterns a tiny twitch when a steadily rising fish continues to ignore my artificial.

I also know that this new method will never make me into the perfect fly fisherman, either. But with these new patterns and this unorthodox presentation, I am now catching several times as many trout from hard-fished waters as I did a few years ago. Try them yourself this coming season during a caddis or stonefly hatch or during those all-too-long "nonhatches." I think they'll do the same for you.

1973

23

Special Deliveries

Switching flies can sometimes change
your luck, but changing your presentation
is usually more killing.

Probably the biggest mistake we fly fishers make—and this includes so-called experts as well as mediocre anglers—is that we stick to one or two tried-and-true presentation methods 99 percent of the time. I even know a few otherwise excellent anglers who fish the dry fly exclusively, no matter what the conditions. When the fish aren't taking, we tend to think that a change of fly pattern is a cure-all when, actually, only a change in presentation will solve the problem.

Except when we're swimming a streamer during high-water conditions, we usually present our flies with upstream casts. And why not? For decades, the experts have agreed that the dead-drift dry fly is the most killing tactic when trout are surface-feeding and that the upstream, weighted nymph is the most productive method when fish seem glued to the bottom. It's all too easy to convince ourselves that we're being smart by playing the percentages.

The only fly in this ointment, as you may have discovered, is that there are times neither of these basic presentations works—

despite their endorsement by the authorities. The main reason for such failures is that heavily pounded trout have seen an endless flotilla of floaters overhead and a steady procession of nymphs bumping them on their noses. Fish can get just as turned off by the same old presentation as they can get fed up with the same old fly pattern. After being pricked, or caught-and-released several times, they're just not having any more.

Yet you don't have to travel to wilderness waters to make decent catches. What you need to do is to travel your flies in a different—though still natural—manner. What are these alternate presentations? Let's start at the top with the dry fly and work our way on down.

It has recently become a well-accepted practice to give a dry caddis-fly imitation an occasional twitch—preferably in an across-and-upstream direction—to imitate the flutterings of the egg-layers. But few anglers ever do this with their mayfly patterns, even though many mayflies, especially the larger species, frequently have difficulty getting airborne and hop and skitter before taking off.

Whenever a good, regularly rising trout refuses my dead-drift imitation a dozen times or more, I wade up slightly above and across from him. Then I cast my fly about two feet above his lie and just twinkle it in the surface film with a slight twitch of my rod tip. Although this same floater failed to fool the fish on its own merits previously, the slight jiggle declares that it is, at least, alive and that's often a clincher.

There are even times and places that call for a nearly straight, downstream dry-fly presentation. Snags or trees that have toppled into the river are choice hangouts for trout. Often the only way you can get a floater to such fish is by drifting it down from upcurrent.

The very tail-ends of pools are usually best fished from above, too. At dusk, good fish tend to drop down-pool to sip spent flies; a favorite lie for such feeding is where the water starts to speed up and break into a riffle. If you try to cover a fish at the bottom lip of a pool from below, the faster water near you will snatch your fly line. This is sure to hurry your fly, causing it to furrow the surface and alarm the fish.

In both situations it's best to cast mainly, but not directly, downstream. Stand five or so feet to one side of a straight, downcurrent line and stop your rod abruptly at the vertical on the foreward cast. This will put enough slack waves in your line so that your fly will float down to the fish drag-free. If the fly floats past the fish, untaken, tighten the line and let the fly swing directly below you, off to one side of the fish. Then you can pick it off the water to recast without spooking the fish.

M·C·WEILER

Then there's an old, but nearly forgotten, way to prospect for trout with an activated floater. Remember Edward R. Hewitt's Never-sink skaters? These flies were tied with oversized hackles on small, light-wire hooks. Hewitt used to twitch these erratically across the surface on slow, deep pools and he used to raise some real busters this way, even during the bright of the day. I haven't seen any Hewitt skaters in tackle shops for decades, but a big, well-greased variant on a smallish hook performs nearly as well. Dun and ginger-grizzly are my favorite colors. Give this trick a try some time when your favorite pool seems utterly dead. You're likely to get the surprise of your life.

The old-fashioned, winged wet fly is worth retrying, too. While its down-and-across-stream swing may not be as killing as the deep-drifted nymph on individual fish, it lets you cover much more water. And overcivilized trout aren't used to seeing artificials behaving this way these days.

Perhaps the deadliest of all wet-fly presentations is the dancing dropper. This technique won't work on the slow water of pools, but it can be murder on fast runs and pocket water.

This is the technique of dancing a dropper-fly downcurrent that was described in detail on pages 169–170.

Don't give up too quickly on obvious hot spots. Tantalize the trout. A dry-fly cast upstream on such water will float past a fish in about half a second and he may, or may not, snatch your artificial. But a juicy, pulsing fly that hovers over his head for thirty seconds or more is usually too big a tease to be ignored.

Nymphs, too, can be fished in different and enticing ways. A deep, dead-drift nymph imitates an immature insect that has been dislodged or is migrating downstream. But what about nymphs and caddis pupae that are rising to the surface to hatch out? And isn't this the time when trout feed on them most eagerly?

To imitate these upwardly mobile insects, much the same technique has been worked out independently on both sides of the Atlantic. Streamkeeper Frank Sawyer on Britain's Hampshire Avon developed the "induced take" and the legendary Jim Leisenring of Pennsylvania limestone country gave us what is now known as the "Leisenring lift," which is described on page 167. This apparently hatching fly will frequently tempt a fish that has ignored the same pattern when dead-drifted past him.

You can even exaggerate this rising action to fool trout that are taking emerging caddis—flies that usually zip to the surface much more abruptly than mayflies do. Position yourself directly above a rising fish, or nearly so. Cast your fly off to one side of him to get his exact measure then haul in a foot of line.

Now cast directly at the fish, but stop your rod suddenly at the vertical as you did when casting a dry fly downstream. This will land your fly only halfway to the trout and it will start sinking immediately on the slack line. When your line goes tight, your fly will rise vertically and quickly right in front of the fish's nose. Only the most blasé trout can ignore a fly behaving like this.

Whether you choose a nymph or a caddis-pupa imitation, your artificial will be more effective if it has been weighted with lead wire under the body dressing. The deeper your offering has sunk before it reaches the fish, the greater will be its upward rise—and its temptation.

Even your minnow-imitating flies, which are usually fished mechanically, across-and-down with a twitch-retrieve, can benefit from an occasional change of pace. One of the most productive streamer-fly fishermen I know often uses his favorite fly in dead-low water. He casts tiny inch-long patterns directly upstream and draws them back just slightly faster than the current. He claims this often stirs up fish that have ignored his nymphs and dries.

Years ago, I discovered—due to a freak accident—a totally different way to present a bucktail.

I was fishing a twenty-five-foot-wide stream not fifty miles from the Empire State Building—one which produced mostly small, stocked fish. But it did have one pool, a deep hole below a plank dam, that I was convinced held bigger, perhaps even wild, trout. The only trouble with this paradise was that it was lined with willows along each bank which made covering the water difficult. The only way I could fish this stretch was to inch upstream, belly-button deep and, even then, the willows, brushing my back, limited my presentation to roll-casting. I rarely saw rises in this deep water, so I usually fished it with a bucktail feeling that "big fly, big fish" was the smart play here.

One evening, during that split-second while my fly was racing along the surface before rolling up and over, a trout savaged that bucktail not five feet in front of me. Why my vintage bamboo rod didn't shatter, I'll never know. But I landed that fish, a solid sixteen-incher, and still my personal best for that stream.

I realized this strike was a once-in-a-lifetime occurrence. But I tried to figure out why that fish had slashed at my fly. There were two reasons, I concluded. First, a terrified baitfish racing along the surface was obviously being chased by another trout and the old carnivore wanted to get there first. And second, he had no time to "stop, look, and listen" before some reflex was triggered.

Admittedly, I have never experienced another take halfway through a roll-cast. But I have put together a presentation that recreates the actions that made that fish strike. And it works often enough so that I still give it a try before I leave a slow, deep hole.

I can't possibly hand-strip a fly fast enough to keep it skittering on top. So what I do is cast my bucktail across-stream and, the instant my fly hits the water, I raise my rod rapidly, wobbling the tip from side to side to give the fly a zigzag pattern along the surface.

Obviously, there are severe limitations to this technique. I can't keep the fly on top if I have more than thirty to thirty-five feet of line out. And I can't make the fly travel this way for more than eight or nine feet before I run out of rod-length. The entire presentation lasts little more than a second. But that short sprint across the surface is often enough to nail a really good fish.

Needless to say, this odd-ball presentation doesn't always work. Neither do any of the other unconventional techniques I've described.

I'm fully resigned to the fact that neither I, nor anyone else, for that matter, will be able to fool all of the fish all of the time. But my fishing diary tells me that when I use a wider variety of presentation methods, I really do fool more of the trout more of the time.

1994

24

Picking Pockets

The biggest fish may inhabit deep pools, but you'll catch more prime, wild ones in pocket-water. Here's how.

Fly fishermen are too often suckered in by picture-book pools. These waters sing us siren songs of huge trout and we tend to cast over them, slavishly, hour after hour.

It's not that the biggest trout in the stream don't live in the deep holes. It's just that you and I aren't about to catch them. Maybe once in an angler's lifetime—if he's lucky—one of those old cannibals will tip up and suck in a #14 Light Cahill. But I'm convinced we'd be better off leaving the slow, deep water to live-bait and night fishermen—except, perhaps, for two fairly brief periods.

During the first two or three weeks of the season, when waters are frigid, pools may offer the only game in town. Trout overwinter in the deepest pools, and that's about the only place you'll find them on opening day.

But when the water warms up into the 50s, trout scatter all over the stream. And once thermometer readings climb into the high 60s, fast water acts like a magnet. Warm water contains far less oxygen than cold does, so trout need swifter flows to increase water traffic through their gills. And faster currents deliver more items of drift food per second to satisfy their growing appetites.

Fish that have remained in slow water stay hidden most of the day. The flat surface overhead offers no concealment. As a result, fly anglers get a shot at them only for a few minutes just before pitch darkness.

During the warm weather that makes up some three-quarters of our open season, you'll catch far more trout if you spend most of your time on runs and pockets. Riffles have fast flows, but they don't provide enough cover to hold decent-sized trout. Runs, with their greater depth, are a better bet. Best of all, though, are the stretches called pocket water, which are just fast-water runs with one important extra. They're studded with large, emerging boulders, which break up the current flows and create a series of minipools.

During floods, water plunges over the tops of boulders and scours out deep holes directly below them. At summer levels, these same boulders break the current, creating eddy pools with slow water directly below them. Here, trout can hold with a minimum of effort and dart out briefly into the faster flows to pick off passing morsels of food. And they can find sanctuary beneath the undercut base of the rock when threatened. In warm weather, a well-scoured pocket is as near to heaven as any trout is likely to get.

Some dry-fly fishermen are put off by pocket water because abrupt changes in water speed caused by braiding currents spell almost instant drag for their fly. Don't worry too much about that. Pocket-water trout aren't nearly as drag-shy as pool-dwellers are. A free float of two feet or so is all you'll need here. Fish hit the fly almost instantly. If you finish off your cast with your rod tip high, so that your fly hits the surface first with most of your line and leader off the water, you should regularly get the necessary few feet of free float.

The most common mistake when fishing dry flies in this type of water is casting too long a line. This is an open invitation to instant drag. Though you may need casts of forty feet or more to keep from alarming trout in smooth water, you can nearly step on them in the crinkled currents of pockets. A twenty-five-foot, upstream cast here should be the maximum, and you'll catch more fish if you limit yourself to twenty or less.

One of the best ways to fish pockets is with a large, dry fly. Bulky-looking patterns like Wulffs, Irresistibles, or Variants are just the ticket. Midges won't work here. You have to offer the trout something meaty enough to make the roundtrip to the surface seem worthwhile. And you won't need a gossamer tippet, either. Sensible 3- or 4-pound test works fine on this roughened water.

Start in just below the most downstream pocket and explore its small area carefully. Make your first casts directly upstream to the tail end of the pocket where the two currents from each side of the boulder join again and start to pick up speed. If there's a hatch of flies or fish are eager to feed, this is the prime spot.

Then work each of the two currents in turn, gradually lengthening your casts until you've covered the water on each side of the boulder itself. Exactly where fish will lie will vary from pocket to pocket, so cover all likely water. The most difficult spot to fish is the back eddy right behind the rock. Violent drag is almost certain and nearly instantaneous here, but pop your fly in there anyway. Once in a while a good fish will chase your skittering offering and savage it.

As you're moving up to the next pocket, pay your parting respects to the boulder. There's often a cushion of dead water right in front of the rock and, if this is the case, an exceptional trout will take over the lie. It pays to make several casts three to four feet directly above the dead center of the boulder before leaving.

Fishing a stretch of pocket water will take you on a zigzag path upriver because you'll cover each pocket most efficiently by casting straight upstream. Wading through the strong currents and over an uneven bottom isn't the easiest going, but you'll be just inching along so it shouldn't be too tiring.

Your casting arm is another matter. This type of fishing calls for rapid-fire presentations. Your fly hits the water, floats a second or so, is snatched off the surface with a roll cast, false-casted a couple of times, then popped out again with your rod tip held high.

Since only a short amount of line is being cast, your rod motions are bunched tightly together. After a while, this staccato routine could wear out the arm of a blacksmith. Take a healthy break between pockets; otherwise, fishing them can become a chore.

You could cover this water in exactly the same manner with a nymph, but that wouldn't spare your arm much, and somehow it's not as productive. Even a weighted nymph barely sinks during such a short travel, so the fish has to rise about the same distance for the fly anyway.

Conventional wet or streamer patterns aren't good choices, either. Sunken flies fished across-stream or across-and-down will sprint, stop dead for a moment, then whip through the water again. They'll be going either too fast or too slow to fish effectively.

There is, however, one lazy man's way to cover this water, and I'm not sure it's not my favorite. I wish I could lay claim to having invented this ingenious method, but I'm afraid it's as old as fly fishing itself—just nearly forgotten. Again, this is the technique of dancing a dropper downstream that I described earlier on pages 169–170.

Though pocket water seldom contains fish you'll want to rush to the taxidermist, it doesn't pester you with small fish, either. A good pocket lie is so choice that it is usually commanded by a sizable specimen. Trout are highly territorial, and mature fish don't suffer small nerds gladly. Most trout you'll catch in this water will run from ten to sixteen inches, with an occasional one stretching to eighteen. This size may not impress spring-creek regulars, but on rain-fed rivers, trout bigger than this have almost always given up an insect diet for minnows and crawfish.

Another plus for pocket water is that you'll usually find more elbowroom there. Tricky currents and tough wading seem to discourage most anglers. I've often had a string of pockets all to myself while the water level in the pool below seemed to rise visibly as angler after angler stepped in.

Then there's the opportunity to stretch a fishing day. As mentioned, slow-water stretches—flats or pools—produce well in summer only during a brief period just before darkness falls, and that's hardly worth a long, roundtrip drive. Pocket water, in all but the hottest weather, usually gives you a couple of productive hours in the morning and, after a midday lull, several more hours after 4 or 5 P.M.

Finally, there's the seldom-mentioned matter of the quality of your catch. Fishermen tend to describe their successes in terms of numbers and lengths. They rarely say whether the fish were wild or freshly stocked. Hatchery fish, after a lifetime of soft living, tend to huddle in slow water and seldom venture up into fast runs and pockets.

Last August, I was invited for an afternoon and evening of fishing at a private club. It owns a lovely stretch of a small river which is grossly overstocked with thirteen- to fifteen-inch hatchery fish. I could count on the toes of one foot the number of wild trout I'd caught there on previous outings. Still, it doesn't hurt the old ego a bit to catch too many biggish trout every once in a while, so I accepted, gratefully.

While driving to a section of their water I hadn't fished previously, I spotted a long chute of pocket water. It was strewn with huge, tilting rock slabs as well as the requisite boulders and promised treacherous footing. However, since it was only about four o'clock of a sunny afternoon, it seemed the likeliest place to give up a few fish before the late-evening rise.

The wading was even more atrocious than I'd expected. I did manage to stay dry, though at times I went through a few unrehearsed routines that might have saved vaudeville.

The fishing, on the other hand, was even better than I'd hoped for. Apparently, club members had given this rock jumble a wide berth. It was loaded with trout that acted like they hadn't seen a fly all year. Better still, they'd never seen a hatchery, either. Every one was a butter-yellow, stream-bred brown.

When it came time to record our catch-and-release figures in the club logbook, I saw I hadn't caught the most fish that day. Neither had I landed the longest one. My best was a shade under fourteen inches; all of them were over eleven.

I wouldn't have traded a single one of them for a pool-full of stockers.

1990

PART 5

the future

25

The Trout Fishing
to Come

Think today's fishing is tough
and stingy? You just might be lucky
to be fishing in the 1990s.

Any prediction about the future becomes an enormously elastic subject. A second from now is every bit as much in the "to come" as is some sci-fi scenario of the exploding (or imploding) of the universe, ending all life with either a bang or a whimper.

So I'll take a moderate perspective and confine my forecast to what is likely to happen during your fishing lifetime of the next few decades.

Before even looking at future trout supplies, we should first start counting trout-catchers. All fifty states will continue to increase in population through fertility and immigration (both legal and illegal) in the years ahead. If the same percentage of Americans are attracted to fly fishing for trout, we'll certainly face an increasing overcrowding crisis.

Despite the old saying that "they're not making any more of it," that's not necessarily true of cold-water fisheries. Population growth means an increase in demand for water and more and more large rivers will be impounded for urban and industrial water reservoirs. New York's Delaware, Arkansas' White River, and New Mexico's San Juan are examples of blue-ribbon trout fisheries created by our insatiable desire for showers and toilet-flushings.

On the other hand, many of today's marginal trout waters will be lost. Water abstraction, housing developments, shopping malls, timbering, and the like will surely increase temperatures and pollution, magnify flood-drought cycles, and increase siltation of spawning beds. So, despite the increase in tailwater fisheries, I expect a slight overall loss in total cold-water stream mileage. Not good news, but don't kill the messenger.

As to the numbers of trout to accommodate this increasing army of anglers on a slightly shrinking mileage, there are several possible solutions. Some are sound, others unsound, and again, I'm sorry to report, I fear the latter will prevail.

Probably, the wisest course would involve habitat, or stream, improvement on all but our largest rivers. This would certainly be costly, but is, on the other hand, long-lasting. Many studies have shown that providing overhead cover, depth, and overwintering holes on small to medium-sized waters can multiply wild trout populations. Perhaps supplemental feeding could even increase this larger head of fish.

More likely, we'll continue the current, short-term, short-sighted policy of stocking hatchery trout. Short-term, because the life-expectancy of a stew-pond trout in a wild river is some two months and almost none overwinter to the next season. Short-sighted, because the gregarious, tank-bred stockers harass the territorial, wild-bred trout. Though they easily chase the inferior stockers out of their territories, in doing so wild trout upset their feeding habits and energy output so that they, too, can't put on the necessary fat for themselves to survive the rigors of winter. The end result is a net loss for both groups of fish.

This self-defeating fishery policy was exposed by Dick Vincent, a Montana state biologist, over twenty years ago. When he stopped stocking a major section of the Madison River (a freestoner), the size and numbers of trout increased nearly 150 percent during the next few years under the same angling regulations. When he started stocking again, size and numbers fell off dramatically. He then tried the same experiment on a nearby private spring creek. Again, stocking, due to the social disruption caused by the hatchery fish, caused a dramatic drop in both fish size and numbers. Once stocking ceased, the fishery rebounded to its former abundance.

Due to these controlled experiments (populations were verified by electro-fishing), Montana does virtually no stream stocking today and yet, despite enormous fishing pressure, the state offers the most and best trout fishing south of the Canadian border. Neighboring Colorado has also reduced stocking to a bare minimum. Why haven't other states followed suit in the face of such evidence?

A few years ago, I would have predicted a spread of this wild-trout policy. Even Trout Unlimited took up the cause for a while.

The reasons why most states stick with their status-quo stocking policies are two-fold. First, they have huge investments in hatchery facilities and a major portion of their annual budgets fund personnel and feed to operate them. After some hundred years of uninterrupted stocking, it's hard to admit that you may have been throwing license-money down the drain for years. I have asked the biologists in my state to stop stocking one blue-ribbon stream for a few years to find out what this policy does to its trout populations. So far this experiment hasn't been carried out. I suspect they're worried about what they might find out.

The second, and principal, cause of continued stocking, however, is purely political. If some, perhaps most, states were to announce they were going to stop stocking trout in their streams, there'd be a scream heard around the world. The rubber-booted, Prince-Albert-can-toting members of the many local "sportsman's" clubs want their fish under their favorite bridge in April and May. Never mind that these eight-inch warriors are flabby and barely fit to eat. Anglers believe their license entitles them to their ten-a-day limit and the state better provide this—or else!

The simple reason why most of our streams are managed for the fishermen rather than for the fish is that the state head of Fish and Wildlife is usually appointed by the governor as a political plum. If an army of angry anglers stormed the state capitol, the top wildlife executive would have to turn in his swivel chair in an instant.

You won't avoid this plague of synthetic fish by joining a private fishing club, either. Clubs are run to keep their lowest common denominator happy. If a member doesn't catch a lot of fish during his few annual visits, he soon becomes a dropout. Most private preserves are even bigger stocking offenders than states.

To maintain a decent head of fish in our rivers for this growing army of anglers, limits will have to become tougher. Whether this will be best accomplished by slot limits, one trophy fish only, or outright no-kill may depend on the size and quality of the fishery in question. But there's no question about it, we'll all be eating less *truite sautée munière* in the future.

No-kill fisheries, or nearly no-kill ones, appear to be the solution, but it may not be as simple as that. It's true that trout can be recycled—but only up to a certain point.

The Brits feel that a released fish is virtually unrecapturable, and most of their clubs stipulate that every legal-sized trout must be creeled until the limit is reached. And they frown on casting to any fish under the size limit. However, they may be as far off the mark as we are.

I've discovered that a middle position, at least with wild trout, is closer to reality. For several years I tagged every over-nine-inch trout I caught on a private stretch of stream with sequentially numbered dorsal tags. I found that four or five recaptures was tops with three relandings nearer to par over the entire season.

I then phoned Charlie Fox on Pennsylvania's Letort because I'd heard he'd been jaw-tagging his trout for years. His results turned out to be similar to mine. Three or four recaptures a season was distinctly good. So it appears that, though trout are, indeed, recyclable, there are severe limits on their reuse.

The only other trout-conserving program I can think of would be to limit fisherman access to blue-ribbon rivers through a lottery the way western elk-hunters are. This plan has been considered on a few slow, weedy streams where excess traffic is scrubbing the bottom clean of insect-and-shrimp-bearing weeds, but, as far as I know, it has yet to be adopted. However, some such restrictions may be imposed on some waters in the future.

Now where does all this leave us? What can we expect, realistically?

There will certainly be more fly fishers on our streams. The solitary experience will become increasingly rare and has already virtually disappeared on our most popular rivers.

Unfortunately, sound, long-range habitat improvement is unlikely to take place, so we can't look there for fish increases. My home state, for example, cut all such projects out of its budget two decades ago. Wild fisheries may continue to exist on a very few private streams, but don't expect to find them on public or fishing-club waters.

There will certainly be tighter creel limits and more of our rivers will be restricted to no-kill rules. Such restrictions may help maintain a reasonable head of trout, but most of the fish will be extremely difficult to catch. I already know of several no-kill fisheries where the trout are virtually uncatchable after mid-June except for a very short period just at dark or when they're on a rare feeding orgy.

There's an old, and probably true, saying that 10 percent of the fishermen catch 90 percent of the trout. My guess is that those figures may soon change to 5 percent catching 95 percent.

If you want to stay in the game, you'd better start to read, study, and practice, practice, practice. In a couple of decades, only the most skillful and knowledgeable fly fishers will be catching trout with any regularity. But isn't that the way it ought to be? After all, fly fishing for trout isn't supposed to compete with the party-boat slaughter of bluefish. That's precisely what makes our sport so absorbing. No other form of angling so decisively rewards excellence and punishes mediocrity.

1995

26

Far from the Maddening Crowd— But Not Very

Where, and how, to find casting room or, at least, unspooked trout amid the coming crowds.

While fly-fishing expertise will hold the key to successful trouting in the future, some sheer animal cunning will come in handy, too. Even a wizard with the fly rod won't take any trout after they've been hounded out of their feeding lies into deep, dark sanctuaries.

But how, and where, will you find fishing elbowroom on increasingly crowded water? There are already several million trouters in America and not nearly that many miles of good—or even decent— public trout streams.

One often written-up method involves checking out topographic maps for far-from-road mountain brooks. While these waterways seldom contain trout over six inches long, there is always the hope that you'll find a beaver pond up this trickle that holds plump, ten- to twelve-inchers.

The only trouble with this scenario is that slogging up steep ravines is punishing exercise. And all too often, you discover after your ordeal that the beavers have decided that the trip wasn't worth the effort long before you did.

Then, too, there is still some true wilderness fishing in parts of Canada and Alaska—but not near any town. Even in Alaska, any stream reachable by a pickup truck has been nearly fished out and is likely to be crowded. There are still plenty of fish out there in remote, roadless areas, but you can reach these only by bush plane. And the costs of such charters—after you've shelled out for air travel, meals, and lodging—make far-north fishing a rare dream-trip rather than a regular routine for most of us.

Let's face it: Most of us have to find trout fishing within a day's or, at most, a weekend's reasonable drive from home. And, if you happen to live in, or near, a big city, you face an extra challenge. I have counted over thirty anglers on one hundred-yard-long pool that's a full three-hour drive from my urban home. While I don't expect a solitary experience on weekends, I do want to avoid areas where all the trout are already cowering under rock slabs before I get there.

My first step is to get a map of the river I'm going to fish (even a road map will do) and locate the stretches that are farthest from

the road. While such areas won't be deserted, the farther in you hike, the fewer fishermen you'll meet.

Even so, you're only halfway home. Though your hike in may have separated the men from the boys, you're more than likely to find one of these men already staked out in the choicest spots.

You still have a shot at good fishing, though. While the earlier and luckier angler may be homesteading the honey spot where the chop from the run above slows and spreads out into deeper water, just think of the places where he *isn't*. Above and below him will be some deep runs and stretches of pocket water. These might not have been your first choices, but they have hidden values. Very likely they haven't been disturbed all day and you may well end up with a better catch than that heron hogging the hot spot.

There are other places fishermen often neglect—at least when they're not packed in shoulder to shoulder. One of my favorites is the very tailend of a pool, just above where the water quickens into the run below.

I'll admit I wouldn't waste a minute on such thin water in mornings or early afternoons. But the hour before dark, when good fish often drop down-pool for the easy feeding on dead or dying egg-layers, pool-tails can turn into hot spots.

The drill here is to wade out quietly into position and stand there, still as a post, until you start to see dimples on the surface. Tie on a spent-wing artificial—one that has the hackle clipped top and bottom so it will lie flat in the surface film like a dead, spread-winged mayfly. Fish it utterly drag-free, nearly upstream; I think you'll be surprised at the size of some of the fish that make rise-forms you'd expect from a three-inch dace.

Another strategy that will nearly always win you more casting room is to fish a stretch from either the difficult, or the "wrong," side. The side of a pool or run where the wading is treacherous or the backcast is restricted draws few customers. Similarly, nearly everyone will fish a bend by casting from the slack inside toward the deeper, faster current on the outside rim.

In both cases, you'll need more effort and skill, and you probably won't be covering quite as many fish. On the other hand, the ones lying on your side of the thread of the current—whether you're casting a dry fly, nymph, or streamer—are unlikely to have been covered earlier that day and they'll be more vulnerable to a fly presented from this seldom-fished side.

I have one, last, crowd-dodging tip for you, even though it applies to only a few special locations. More and more streams, or sections of them, are being limited to no-kill status. Fishery managers have found this to be an effective way to keep enough mature, wild breeding stock in a river to assure its future.

Most anglers figure, and rightly so, that the places where no trout are being taken out have to hold the most fish. As a result, such set-aside sections draw by far the biggest crowds.

If one of the rivers near you has such restricted sections, you can often cash in on this. Just fish a half-mile or so above or below the posted boundaries. These contiguous stretches often hold nearly as many fish as the "no-kill" water. This is because trout are constantly striving to improve their station in life. When a big fish is unwillingly removed from his choice lie or feeding station, you can bet that another one from nearby will move in quickly.

Of course, none of the above strategies will earn you either a solitary or wilderness experience. But they will give you more breathing room and a better shot at trout that are less harried and suspicious.

You can complain all you like about crowded conditions, but you'll be doing so from the tailend of a very long line. Over four hundred years ago, the Elizabethan poet Thomas Bastard was lamenting that "fishes decrease and fishers multiply."

Let's face it: trout will become scarcer, competition more plentiful, and trout-catching tougher. I can only hope that the unorthodox fly patterns, strategies, tactics, and techniques recommended in this book will help you meet, and surmount, this increasing challenge.

1995